WALES
Bed & Breakfast

WALES CYMRU

Llynnau Mymbyr, Snowdonia

THE *Best* CHOICE

Bed & Breakfast accommodation has come a long way since the old days when proprietors simply hung a sign up on the door and hoped for the best. Today's B&Bs can be very well equipped indeed, with full en-suite facilities and comfortable accommodation often matching good hotel standards.

But they haven't lost their price advantage. The highest price you'll find in this book is just £25 per person per night. And that's the top rate – most places cost even less.

You'll find a great choice of B&Bs between these covers, based at small hotels, inns, guest houses, farmhouses and private homes throughout Wales. It's a friendly form of accommodation which combines great value with comfort and high standards – and usually good home cooking into the bargain.

And you can make your choice safe in the knowledge that all the accommodation featured is subject to the Wales Tourist Board's Quality Assurance schemes, backed up by regular inspection visits. This publication is committed to quality – you'd expect nothing less from the Wales Tourist Board's official guide to B&B.

Contents

Mawddach Estuary, Mid Wales

GRADES & CROWNS Explained

All the accommodation in this book has been inspected and graded by the Wales Tourist Board. The WTB's Quality Assurance schemes are your passport to an enjoyable holiday. The schemes help pinpoint the type of accommodation that's just right for you, for we spell out clearly the quality and standards on offer. And you can book with confidence, for all the accommodation featured is regularly visited by WTB inspectors to make sure that standards are being maintained.

Making the Grade

Look out first for the **GRADES** – they're your guide to the **QUALITY** of the comfort and service you can expect.

APPROVED	**Good**
COMMENDED	**Very Good**
HIGHLY COMMENDED	**Excellent**
DE LUXE	**A special accolade representing exceptional comfort and service**

Grades are an assessment of <u>**overall quality**</u> based on the welcome, service and standards provided, taking into account the nature and size of the establishment. Therefore you will find that properties with limited facilities and only a few Crowns (see opposite) might well achieve the Highly Commended or De Luxe quality grade.

Focus on Facilities

Then there are **CROWNS**, which tell you how **WELL EQUIPPED** the accommodation is. The more facilities, the higher the Crown rating.

There are six categories:

WELCOME HOME

Usually smaller establishments with clean and comfortable accommodation and a reasonable range of facilities and services

Additional facilities, including washbasin in bedroom

Some bedrooms with bath (or shower) and WC. Colour TV in bedroom or lounge. Guests can enjoy morning tea/coffee in bedroom

At least 50% of bedrooms with bath (or shower) and WC en-suite. Hot evening meal available

90% of bedrooms with bath (or shower) and WC en-suite. TV, radio and telephone in all bedrooms. Evening meals can be ordered up to 10.30pm. Lounge service until midnight

All bedrooms with bath, fixed shower and WC en-suite. Restaurant open for breakfast, lunch and dinner. All-night lounge service and night porter on duty

Please Note

All Gradings, Awards and Classifications were correct at the time of going to press. Inspections are on-going and improvements made by establishments may have resulted in a revision since publication. Please check when booking. Further information on the Grading, Award and Crown schemes is available from:

Trade and Consumer Relations Dept
Wales Tourist Board
Brunel House
2 Fitzalan Road
Cardiff CF2 1UY
Tel (01222) 475281
Fax (01222) 475319

E-mail: info@tourism.wales.gov.uk

Internet site:
www.tourism.wales.gov.uk

USING THIS GUIDE

Here's a typical entry, which tells you what to look out for when choosing your accommodation. Please note that the explanations are based on the way we display a **standard** entry in the following 'where to stay' advertising section. For the **smallest** style of entry there will be minor changes to the way in which the information is presented.

Type of Accommodation

GH indicates Guest House

H indicates Hotel

FH indicates Farmhouse

FGH indicates Farm Guest House

Descriptive Copy

Please note:
The descriptive wording in each accommodation entry has been provided by the proprietors

Key to Symbols

P Private car parking/garage facilities at establishment

Dogs/pets accepted into establishment by arrangement

C Children under 12 accommodated free if sharing parents' room (meals charged extra)

Liquor licence

Central heating throughout

Evening meals available by prior arrangement

Totally non-smoking establishment

Areas provided for smokers

Please note: Symbols are based on information provided by the proprietors

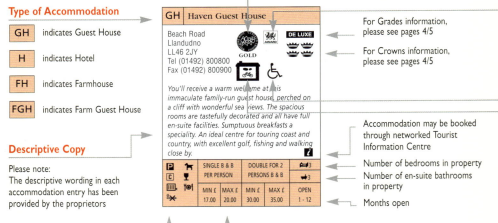

GH | Haven Guest House

Beach Road
Llandudno
LL46 2JY
Tel (01492) 800800
Fax (01492) 800900

GOLD DE LUXE

You'll receive a warm welcome at this immaculate family-run guest house, perched on a cliff with wonderful sea views. The spacious rooms are tastefully decorated and all have full en-suite facilities. Sumptuous breakfasts a speciality. An ideal centre for touring coast and country, with excellent golf, fishing and walking close by.

P		SINGLE B & B		DOUBLE FOR 2		3
C		PER PERSON		PERSONS B & B		3
		MIN £	MAX £	MIN £	MAX £	OPEN
		17.00	20.00	30.00	35.00	1 - 12

For Grades information, please see pages 4/5

For Crowns information, please see pages 4/5

Accommodation may be booked through networked Tourist Information Centre

Number of bedrooms in property

Number of en-suite bathrooms in property

Months open

Prices

Single rates are for ONE PERSON in a single room. Double rates are for TWO PEOPLE sharing a double or twin room. There may be supplements for private bath/shower and single occupancy of a double/twin room. All prices quoted include VAT at the current rate (17.5%). Prices and other specific holiday information in this publication were supplied to the Wales Tourist Board during June–September 1997. So do check all prices and facilities before confirming your booking.

The maximum you'll pay for B&B accommodation in this guide is £25 per person. You'll find that most rates quoted are even less.

Welcome Host

The Wales Tourist Board's Welcome Host scheme encourages the highest standards of customer care, placing the emphasis on hospitality, friendliness and first-class service. There are two categories:

 At least 90% of staff are participants

GOLD

 At least 50% of staff are participants

Award Winners (applicable to farmhouses/guest houses only)

 Look out also for this symbol if you want extra-special farm or guest house accommodation. It is only given to establishments which have won the coveted Wales Tourist Board Award. All Award winners will have the Highly Commended or De Luxe grade. In addition, proprietors will have successfully completed the Welcome Host Manager Course as well as an approved course in farm-based tourism or guest house management.

Walkers and Cyclists Welcome

 Walking and cycling enthusiasts should look out for this sign, which includes the 'foot' and/or 'bike' symbols. It's displayed by places which have undertaken to provide features which walkers and cyclists always find welcome – drying facilities for wet clothes and boots, secure lockable areas for bikes, adequate storage space for rucksacks, packed lunches and so on.

Accommodating Wheelchair Users

Properties are assessed for access by wheelchair users. Those suitable will have one of the following grades:

 Accessible to a wheelchair user travelling independently

 Accessible to a wheelchair user travelling with assistance

 Accessible to a wheelchair user able to walk a few paces and up a maximum of three steps

For further details, please see 'Information for Visitors with Disabilities' in the 'Further Information/Useful Addresses' section of this guide.

The pretty resort and sailing centre of Aberdovey

BOOKING
Information

Book Direct

Telephone or write to the place of your choice direct. It's as simple as that. If you phone, please check the prices and follow up the call with a letter of confirmation enclosing whatever deposit you've agreed with the proprietor.

Book through a TIC

Look out for this symbol on the following pages. It means that you can book the featured accommodation through any networked Tourist Information Centre. Please see the TIC list at the back of this guide for more details on this Bed Booking Service.

Children Stay Free

Many hotels, guest houses and farmhouses offer free accommodation for children under 12 if sharing their parents' room (you only pay for their meals). It's always worth asking about reductions, for most operators will offer child discounts. Family holiday hotels, especially in major resorts, also cater for one-parent families.

Deposits

Most operators will ask for a deposit when a reservation is being made. Some establishments may request payment in advance of arrival.

Cancellation and Insurance

When you confirm a holiday booking, please bear in mind that you are entering a legally binding contract which entitles the proprietor to compensation if you fail to take up the accommodation. It's always wise to arrange holiday insurance to cover you for cancellation and other unforeseen eventualities. If you have to alter your travel plans, please advise the holiday operator or proprietor immediately.

Any Problems?

We care about our visitors' views and encourage you to make any comments you may have about your stay to the proprietor of the establishment at the time of your visit. In this way it may be possible to make your stay even more pleasurable and to arrange for new facilities and services to be provided in the future.

If you need to get in touch with the Wales Tourist Board about any aspect of your stay please contact:

**Trade and Consumer Relations Dept
Wales Tourist Board
Brunel House
2 Fitzalan Road
Cardiff CF2 1UY
Tel (01222) 475281/475278**

We will let you have a reply to your letter or call within 15 working days of its receipt.

BWRDD CROESO CYMRU
WALES TOURIST BOARD

WHEN AN
Inspector Calls

We're often asked how we measure quality at B&Bs. Teams of inspectors are out and about in Wales assessing hotels, guest houses and farmhouses on an annual basis for the Approved, Commended, Highly Commended or De Luxe grade. If you think it's an easy life, then read on.

First, the inspector makes a telephone booking, never revealing his or her identity. Even at this early stage, the property is under examination. Initial impressions are so important, and the way in which the reservation is handled forms the first stage of the grading procedure.

When the inspector arrives, first impressions are again crucial – the neatness and look of the property, garden and so on. Then comes the welcome. The warmth of welcome is especially important when grading B&Bs. A typical property will be family run with only a few bedrooms and limited facilities in comparison with, say, a country house hotel. But everything is judged in its proper context. The inspector's assessment is always influenced by the nature of the establishment and style of operation.

So a small B&B can receive a top grade if what it offers is of very high quality.

In the bedroom, the quality of the furniture, décor, carpeting, bathroom accessories, beds, bedlinen and so on are put under the microscope. There has to be a *consistency* of quality. If a room has luxurious furnishings but happens to have an inferior, lumpy bed, then it won't attract a top grade.

The inspector then has to attend to the paperwork. A detailed grading report has to be compiled with supporting comments covering the items already mentioned, together with others such as lighting and heating. These individual marks form the basis of a judgement of the overall quality – and the grade. Breakfast, of course, also plays an important part. Emphasis is placed on freshly cooked breakfasts, home-made jams and marmalades and so on.

At the presentation of the bill, the inspector announces his or her identity. In the words of one old hand, 'It's at that stage that the proprietor faints!' And, for the poor inspector, the whole thing happens again and again – for about 200 days a year.

9

Instant

REFERENCE GUIDE

Page

De Luxe Accommodation (see page 4)

Award-Winning Farms and Guest Houses (see page 7)

Properties for Wheelchair Users (see page 7)

1997 Wales Tourist Board
Tourism Award Winners
Sponsored by Schroders
The Award winners included:

Best Large Tourism Business Award

OAKWOOD PARK

Canaston Bridge, nr Narberth (tel 01834-891376)

Oakwood Park is one of Wales's most popular family attractions, with almost $^1/_2$ million visitors a year. Opened in 1987, it has over 40 rides and amusements including a Western-style gold mining town and exciting water and sky coasters. One of its latest additions is Megafobia, Europe's largest wooden roller coaster.

Best Medium-Sized Business Award

LLANGORSE ROPE CENTRE

Llangorse, near Brecon (tel 01874-658272/658584)

This is a new concept in indoor activity and training, with large natural and artificial rock surfaces, abseil tower and 'cave'. The imaginatively converted farm buildings also features a 9m/30ft pit, rope bridge and tree climb.

Best Small Tourism Business Award

LLANGLOFFAN FARMHOUSE CHEESE CENTRE

Castle Morris, nr Fishguard (tel 01348-891241)

Llangloffan was one of the places responsible for reviving the art of farmhouse cheesemaking in Wales. Llangloffan is a delicious full-fat hard cheese made in the farm's own dairy using traditional equipment and methods. Visitors are welcome to the farmhouse to see the process for themselves (cheesemaking takes place in the mornings).

Environmental Practice Award

ANGLESEY SEA ZOO

Brynseincyn, Isle of Anglesey (tel 01248-430411)

The zoo has exciting live exhibitions of Anglesey's sea life. A major tourist attraction, it has been most successful in its aim of introducing the island's rich marine heritage to a wide audience. The zoo's philosophy is to take away as little as possible from the wild, to put back as much as possible, and to learn to breed wherever possible.

WHERE TO STAY
Finding Your Way Around

It's easy to pinpoint the accommodation you want in this guide. You'll see from the map that we have divided **Wales** into 12 holiday areas. **Within each individual area, the resorts, towns and villages are listed alphabetically. Each place has a map reference enabling you to locate it on the detailed gridded maps at the back of the book.**

Please note that the borders between each area are only approximate. Places on or close to the border may choose to be listed under the area or areas of their choice.

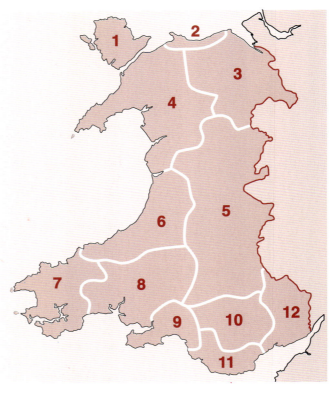

1

Holyhead

Llangefni

Menai Bridge

Beaumaris

Llanfairpwllgwyngell

The Isle of Anglesey

This island is a place of great natural beauty, history and heritage. The coastline is astonishingly varied – from the dunes of Newborough to the sea-cliffs of Holyhead Mountain and the open sands of Red Wharf Bay. Anglesey, with its small, stylish resorts, is the perfect destination for the quieter seaside holiday. If you can drag yourself away from the beach you'll find a huge range of places to visit – ancient burial chambers, the mansion of Plas Newydd, Beaumaris Castle and the award-winning Anglesey Sea Zoo to name but a few.

If you're a birdwatcher, bring your binoculars to the cliffs at South Stack or the sands at Malltraeth. For sailors, there are the sheltered waters of the Menai Strait between Anglesey and the mainland of North Wales.

Plas Newydd

It's a fact...

Opened in 1826, Thomas Telford's elegant bridge spanning the Menai Strait was the world's first large iron suspension bridge. In the 19th century the puffin inhabitants of Puffin Island off the Anglesey coast were caught, filleted, pickled in brine and served as a delicacy. Most of Anglesey's 125-mile coastline has been declared an 'Area of Outstanding Natural Beauty' (designated in 1966). The world-famous town with the longest name is Llanfairpwllgwyngyllgogerychwyrndrobwllllantysiliogogogoch, which means 'St Mary's (Church) by the white aspen over the whirlpool, and St Tysilio's (Church) by the red cave'.

Ad4 Brynsiencyn

Anglesey hamlet near shores of Menai Strait, looking across to Snowdonia. Bodowyr Burial Chamber, Plas Newydd stately home, Anglesey Model Village, Kids and Family attraction, Foel Farm Park, Bryntirion Open Farm, and award-winning Anglesey Sea Zoo all nearby.

Ac1 Cemaes

Quaint unspoilt village with stone quay on rugged northern shores of Anglesey. Boating, fishing and swimming. Wylfa Nuclear Power Station open to the public.

Aa2 Holyhead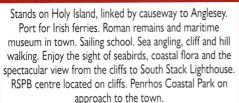

Stands on Holy Island, linked by causeway to Anglesey. Port for Irish ferries. Roman remains and maritime museum in town. Sailing school. Sea angling, cliff and hill walking. Enjoy the sight of seabirds, coastal flora and the spectacular view from the cliffs to South Stack Lighthouse. RSPB centre located on cliffs. Penrhos Coastal Park on approach to the town.

Ab2 Llanfachraeth

Village a mile or so inland from Anglesey's sandy north-western shores. Also close to spectacular cliffs of Holy Island and port of Holyhead.

Ac4 Llangaffo

On an Anglesey crossroads in the south-western corner of the island. Good birdwatching along Malltraeth Sands and Marsh, excellent, spacious beach at Newborough (drive through the forest), award-winning Anglesey Sea Zoo at Brynsiencyn.

Ad3 Llangefni

Market town and shopping centre, Anglesey's administrative 'capital'. Fine touring base; almost all of the island's coastline is within 10-15 mile radius. Many attractions and prehistoric sites nearby. Art gallery with historic displays, sports centre. Trout fishing in nearby Cefni Reservoir.

Ac2 Llannerch-y-medd

Central Anglesey village with easy access to island's beaches. Visit Din Llugwy, ancient remains of fortified village, the working windmill at Llanddeusant and the Llyn Alaw Visitor Centre.

Aa3 Trearddur Bay

Most attractive holiday spot set amongst low cliffs on Holy Island near Holyhead. Golden sands, golf, sailing, fishing, swimming.

South Stack, Isle of Anglesey

Brynsiencyn Cemaes Holyhead Llanfachraeth Llangaffo

GH Fron Guest House

Brynsiencyn
LL61 6TX
Tel: (01248) 430310

HIGHLY COMMENDED

High class traditional bed and breakfast with en-suite facilities in centrally heated guest house. Tea/coffee making tray, TVs, warm family atmosphere. Off road parking. Magnificent views of Snowdonia. Ideally situated for touring Anglesey or mountains. Heated swimming pool with patio from Spring Bank Holiday till end of August.

| P | | SINGLE PER PERSON B&B | | DOUBLE FOR 2 PERSONS B&B | | 🛏 3 |
						🛏 1
		MIN £	MAX £	MIN £	MAX £	OPEN
		18.00	–	32.00	35.00	2-10

H Holland Hotel

LLanfachraeth,
Holyhead
LL65 4UH
Tel: (01407) 740252

COMMENDED

Traditional friendly Welsh village inn, offering three double rooms and one family room, all en-suite. Rare Camra good beer guide recommended, with extensive quality menu including vegetarian dishes. Convenient for day trips to Ireland aboard exciting high speed catamaran ferries. Ample game, sea and course angling plus safe sandy beaches.

| P | | SINGLE PER PERSON B&B | | DOUBLE FOR 2 PERSONS B&B | | 🛏 4 |
						🛏 4
		MIN £	MAX £	MIN £	MAX £	OPEN
		22.00	24.00	44.00	48.00	1-12

GH Wavecrest

93 Newry Street,
Holyhead
LL65 1HU
Tel: (01407) 763637
Fax: (01407) 763637

GOLD COMMENDED

Situated in a quiet location, yet only two minutes from ferry terminal and town centre and close to South Stack. Ideal for break of journey to/from Ireland. We cater for all ferry timings. All rooms furnished to high standard with extra facilities including colour satellite TV, en-suite available including large family room children and pets welcome. AA Recommended.

| | | SINGLE PER PERSON B&B | | DOUBLE FOR 2 PERSONS B&B | | 🛏 4 |
						🛏 2
		MIN £	MAX £	MIN £	MAX £	OPEN
		16.00	–	30.00	36.00	1-12

FH Tyddyn Goblet

Brynsiencyn
LL61 6TZ
Tel: (01248) 430296

AWARD HIGHLY COMMENDED

Character farmhouse set back 200 yards from A4080 Newborough Road. Ground floor en-suite bedrooms with colour television and tea making facilities. Evening dinner optional. Attractive lounge and pleasant dining room with separate tables and lovely open views. 5 miles from Brittania Bridge, convenient for North Wales coast and Snowdonia. Many main Anglesey attractions nearby.
Brochure Mrs Williams.

| P | | SINGLE PER PERSON B&B | | DOUBLE FOR 2 PERSONS B&B | | 🛏 2 |
						🛏 2
		MIN £	MAX £	MIN £	MAX £	OPEN
		15.00	17.00	30.00	34.00	3-11

GH The Monraven Guest House

Porth-y-Felin Road,
Holyhead
LL65 1PL
Tel: (01407) 762944
Fax: (01407) 762944
E-mail: monravon@marketsite.co.uk

COMMENDED

A family-run business offering bed and breakfast with all bedrooms en-suite. 2 minutes to ferry terminals, just off main street. Near beach and park. Very suitable for stopovers before boarding ferries for Ireland. Open 24 hours for late arrivals and departures. Totally non-smoking. This is a peace and quiet establishment where cleanliness is our speciality.

| P | | SINGLE PER PERSON B&B | | DOUBLE FOR 2 PERSONS B&B | | 🛏 5 |
						🛏 5
		MIN £	MAX £	MIN £	MAX £	OPEN
		–	–	32.00	35.00	1-12

FH Penyrorsedd Farm

Llanfachraeth,
Holyhead
LL65 4YB
Tel: (01407) 730630

HIGHLY COMMENDED

A charming 18th century farmhouse full of character, on a 400 acre beef and sheep farm, where guests are assured of a warm and friendly welcome. Traditional Welsh breakfast served to guests own requirements. Conveniently situated for Irish sea crossings. Horseriding, golf and fishing nearby. Just off the A5025, close to sandy beach.

| P | | SINGLE PER PERSON B&B | | DOUBLE FOR 2 PERSONS B&B | | 🛏 3 |
						🛏 2
		MIN £	MAX £	MIN £	MAX £	OPEN
		–	–	36.00	40.00	1-11

GH The Firs

Cemlyn,
Cemaes
LL67 ODU
Tel: (01407) 710622

APPROVED

Open 1-12

B&B pp £15.00 - £17.50. Double, B&B £29.00 - £34.00

P			🛏 5	🛏 –

Prices

In this publication we go to great lengths to make sure that you have a clear, accurate idea of prices and facilities. It's all spelled out in the 'Prices' section - and remember to confirm everything when making your booking.

GH Roselea

26 Holborn Road,
Holyhead
LL65 2AT
Tel: (01407) 764391
Fax: (01407) 764391

GOLD HIGHLY COMMENDED

Homely guest house 2 minutes from ferry, station, beaches, golf course. Ideally situated for fishing, birdwatching, climbing and walking. Tea/coffee, TV all bedrooms. TV lounge. Catering for early-late ferry travellers. Rooms furnished to high standard. We are in the "Which?" Best Bed and Breakfast Guide. Proprietor Mrs S Foxley guarantees personal attention.

| | | SINGLE PER PERSON B&B | | DOUBLE FOR 2 PERSONS B&B | | 🛏 3 |
						🛏 –
		MIN £	MAX £	MIN £	MAX £	OPEN
		18.00	18.00	28.00	28.00	1-12

FGH Plas Llangaffo

Llangaffo
LL60 6LR
Tel: (01248) 440452

APPROVED

Peaceful location near to Newborough Forest and Llandwyn Bay with its miles of golden sands. Large garden for visitors use. Free range eggs and home made marmalade for breakfast. Dinner optional. Horseriding available. Half a mile from cycle route 8, we have bicycles for hire. Ideal as a base to visit Ireland.

| P | | SINGLE PER PERSON B&B | | DOUBLE FOR 2 PERSONS B&B | | 🛏 5 |
						🛏 –
		MIN £	MAX £	MIN £	MAX £	OPEN
		15.00	15.00	30.00	30.00	1-12

Llangefni Llannerch-y-medd Trearddur Bay

GH | Argraig

Llangristiolus,
Bodorgan
LL62 5PW
Tel: (01248) 724390

HIGHLY COMMENDED

GOLD

Homely B&B with twin/double room, with hot/cold, tea/coffee facility, colour TV. Private bathroom. Children welcome. Off road parking. Located half a mile west of the A5 road on the B4422, signposted Aberffraw, first house on the left after village sign of Llangristiolus. Sorry no brochure. A warm Welsh welcome awaits you. Contact Mrs Griffiths.

P C IIII ♿	SINGLE PER PERSON B&B		DOUBLE FOR 2 PERSONS B&B		🛏 1 🛋 1
	MIN £	MAX £	MIN £	MAX £	OPEN
	16.00	16.00	32.00	32.00	3-10

FGH | Drws-y-Coed

Llannerch-y-medd
LL71 8AD
Tel: (01248) 470473

DE LUXE

GOLD

AWARD

Enjoy wonderful panoramic views of Snowdonia at this beautifully appointed farmhouse on a 550 acre working farm. It is situated in peaceful, wooded countryside in the centre of Anglesey. Tastefully decorated en-suite bedrooms with all facilities. Central heating. Inviting spacious lounge with log fire. Games room. Historic farmstead. Lovely private walks. Guests return year after year.

P IIII ✂	SINGLE PER PERSON B&B		DOUBLE FOR 2 PERSONS B&B		🛏 3 🛋 3
	MIN £	MAX £	MIN £	MAX £	OPEN
	25.00	25.00	40.00	45.00	1-12

GH | Moranedd Guest House

Trearddur Road,
Trearddur Bay
LL65 2UE
Tel: (01407) 860324

HIGHLY COMMENDED

Open 1-12

B&B pp £15.00 - £25.00. Double, B&B Max £30.00

P IIII   🛏 6 🛋

WALES TOURIST MAP

- Our best selling map - fully updated and improved for 1998
- Detailed 5 miles/inch scale
- Wealth of tourist information
- Specially devised car tours
- Town plans

£2.35 inc. p&p
(see 'Guides and Maps' at the end of the book)

Trearddur Bay

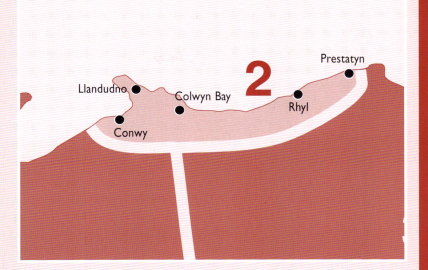

2

Prestatyn

Llandudno

Colwyn Bay

Rhyl

Conwy

North Wales's sandy coastal strip is famous for its popular mixture of big beaches, colourful attractions and family entertainment. But within this formula there's scope for variety. Historic Conwy, with its ancient walls and castle, still retains a medieval air. Llandudno, the stately 'Queen' of the Welsh resorts, remains faithful to its Victorian roots while at the same time catering for the needs of today's visitors. For sheer seaside harmony, there's nothing quite like the view along its seafront from the headland above. Colwyn Bay, Rhyl and

Prestatyn offer unpretentious fun and amusement, with huge beaches and an even larger choice of attractions, including the marvellous Welsh Mountain Zoo (Colwyn Bay), the Sun Centre (Rhyl) and the Nova Centre (Prestatyn).

Rhyl

It's a fact...

Llandudno's pier is over 900m/3000ft long. The resort's alpine-style Cabin Lift, one of the longest in Britain, carries passengers by cablecar for over a mile from the seafront to the summit of the Great Orme headland. Conwy has Britain's 'smallest house', a tiny fisherman's cottage on the quay. The Welsh Mountain Zoo at Colwyn Bay is owned by the Zoological Society of Wales, an educational and scientific charity. Rhyl's 73m-/240ft-high Skytower offers spectacular views from Snowdonia to Liverpool. Prestatyn is at one end of the 168-mile Offa's Dyke Path.

Llandudno, Colwyn Bay, Rhyl and Prestatyn

Bc4 Colwyn Bay

Bustling seaside resort with large sandy beach. Promenade amusements. Good touring centre for Snowdonia. Leisure centre, Eirias Park, Dinosaur World, famous Mountain Zoo with Chimpanzee World. Puppet theatre. Golf, tennis, riding and other sports. Quieter Rhos on Sea at western end of bay.

Bb4 Conwy

Historic town with mighty castle and complete ring of medieval town walls. Dramatic estuary setting. Many ancient buildings including Aberconwy House. Telford Suspension Bridge, popular fish quay, spectacular wall walks. Golf, pony trekking, Butterfly House, art gallery, aquarium, pleasure cruises. Tiny 'smallest house' on quay. Touring centre for Snowdonia.

Bb3 Llandudno

Premier coastal resort of North Wales with everything the holidaymaker needs. Two beaches, spacious promenade, Victorian pier, excellent shopping. Donkey rides, Punch and Judy, ski slope, Alice in Wonderland exhibition, art gallery, museum, old copper mines open to the public, splendid North Wales Theatre. Visit the Great Orme headland above the resort and ride by cabinlift or tramway. Conference centre. Many daily coach excursions. Wales in Bloom winner 1997.

Be3 Prestatyn

Family seaside resort on popular North Wales coast. Entertainment galore at superb Nova Centre including heated swimming pools and aquashute. Sailing, swimming on long, sandy coastline. Close to pastoral Vale of Clwyd and Clwydian Range. At northern end of long-distance Offa's Dyke Path.

Bb3 Rhos on Sea

Attractive seaside village linking Llandudno and Colwyn Bay with promenade, beach, golf, water-skiing, puppet theatre. Colwyn Bay Mountain Zoo nearby.

Bd3 Rhyl

Fun-packed resort offering all-round entertainment. The Sun Centre 'indoor beach' with swimming pool and slides together with 73m/240ft Sky Tower are two major attractions; others include Knight's Caverns, Sea Life Centre, big funfair, Marine Lake, Superbowl, Botanical Gardens. Swimming and sailing. Ideal seaside resort for the whole family. Wales in Bloom winner 1997.

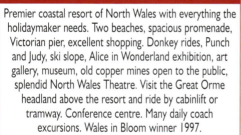

Llandudno

Conwy Castle (top)

GH Crossroads

15 Coed Pella Road,
Colwyn Bay
LL29 7AT
Tel: (01492) 530736

COMMENDED

GOLD

Crossroads is one of the oldest established guesthouses in Colwyn Bay, homely and tasteful, central for all the wonders of North Wales. Just a short drive to visit the mountains, lakes and rivers with a stunning coastline of castles, stately homes, narrow gauge railways. Come and explore this land of myths and legends. En-suite supplement £3.00 per person per night. AAQQ

		SINGLE PER PERSON B&B		DOUBLE FOR 2 PERSONS B&B		🛏 5 🛏 2
P 🐕 🛗		MIN £	MAX £	MIN £	MAX £	OPEN
		13.00	15.00	26.00	30.00	1-12

GH Pen-y-Bryn

Lancaster Square,
Conwy
LL32 8DE
Tel: (01492) 596445

HIGHLY COMMENDED

May we offer guests the unique opportunity of relaxing overnight within the historic town walls of Conwy. Our cosy 16th century tearooms Egon Ronay Recommended, compliment the accommodation ideally. En-suite rooms with central heating, colour TVs and hairdryers. Non-smoking throughout. Private car parking available. Brochure on application. Warm welcome guaranteed.

		SINGLE PER PERSON B&B		DOUBLE FOR 2 PERSONS B&B		🛏 3 🛏 2
P 🐕 🛗 ✗		MIN £	MAX £	MIN £	MAX £	OPEN
		20.00	25.00	32.00	42.00	2-12

FH Henllys Farm

Llechwedd,
Conwy
LL32 8DJ
Tel: (01492) 593269

HIGHLY COMMENDED

AWARD

In the heart of beautiful countryside ideally placed for touring Snowdonia and North Wales coast, Bodnant Garden and Anglesy. One and half miles from Conwy. Twin/double family rooms, both en-suite and tea/coffee making facilities. Guest TV lounge, good home-cooking from fresh local produce. Homely peaceful accommodation with ample secure parking.

		SINGLE PER PERSON B&B		DOUBLE FOR 2 PERSONS B&B		🛏 2 🛏 2
P C 🛗 ✗ 🍽		MIN £	MAX £	MIN £	MAX £	OPEN
		20.00	20.00	32.00	40.00	3-11

H Carmel Private Hotel

17 Craig-y-Don Parade
Promenade
Llandudno
LL30 1BG
Tel: (01492) 877643

HIGHLY COMMENDED

Open 3-10

B&B pp £15.00 - £20.00. Double, B&B £29.00 - £35.00

P 🐕 🛗 ✗ 🍽	🛏 9 🛏 6

H Glenormes Hotel

Central Promenade
Llandudno LL30 1AR
Tel: (01492) 876643

HIGHLY COMMENDED

Seafront Victorian gentlemans residence uniquely situated opposite the beach with glorious uninterrupted bay views. All 12 individual charming en-suite bedrooms have antique furnishings plus heating, TV, hairdryer, toiletries, beverage facilities, biscuits etc. Two superb genuine Victorian four poster bedrooms. Private car park. Easy level walk to shops, restaurants and pier. Glenormes, combining period elegance with modern comfort.

		SINGLE PER PERSON B&B		DOUBLE FOR 2 PERSONS B&B		🛏 12 🛏 12
P 🍷 🛗 ♿ 🍽		MIN £	MAX £	MIN £	MAX £	OPEN
		-	-	44.00	48.00	4-10

H Karden House Hotel

16 Charlton Street,
Llandudno
LL30 2AA
Tel: (01492) 879347

COMMENDED

Open 1-12

B&B pp £13.50 - £14.50. Double, B&B £27.00 - £29.00

🍷 🛗 🍽	🛏 10 🛏 4

H Lynton House Hotel

80 Church Walks,
Llandudno
LL30 2HD
Tel: (01492) 875057/875009
Fax: (01492) 875057

HIGHLY COMMENDED

A small homely hotel fifty yards from the pier, close to the shops, skiing and promonade. All rooms are decorated to a high standard with en-suite bathrooms, colour TV, tea/coffee tray and telephones. Highly recommended home-cooking with a choice of menu, special diets catered for. Four poster rooms including whirlpool bath. Parking.

		SINGLE PER PERSON B&B		DOUBLE FOR 2 PERSONS B&B		🛏 14 🛏 14
P 🐕		MIN £	MAX £	MIN £	MAX £	OPEN
C 🍷		21.00	25.00	42.00	44.00	1-12
🛗 ♿ 🍽						

GH Midshores Hotel

1 Salisbury Road,
Llandudno
LL30 2EG
Tel: (01492) 875819

COMMENDED

Open 3-10

B&B pp £14.00 - £18.00. Double, B&B £28.00 - £36.00

🍷 🛗 ♿ 🍽	🛏 9 🛏 1

H Minion Hotel

21/23 Carmen Sylva Road,
Llandudno
LL30 1EQ
Tel: (01492) 877740

COMMENDED

Open 4-10

B&B pp £15.50 - £17.50. Double, B&B £31.00 - £35.00

P 🐕 🍷 🍽	🛏 12 🛏 12

Rhos on Sea

Llandudno Prestatyn Rhos on Sea Rhyl

H	Tan Lan Hotel

Great Ormes Road,  **HIGHLY COMMENDED**
West Shore, Llandudno
LL30 2AR
Tel: (01492) 860221
Fax: (01492) 870219

'A special find'. Ideal base for touring and local attractions. Warm welcome assured, experience our hospitality. All 17 rooms en-suite, tastefully furnished and decorated. Attentive service combined with friendly atmosphere where you may feel genuinely at home. You can be assured of extraordinarily good food in our restaurant. Ample parking. Brochure sent with pleasure.

P ⚘	SINGLE PER PERSON B&B		DOUBLE FOR 2 PERSONS B&B		🛏17 🛏17
♦ ⏢ 🍴	MIN £	MAX £	MIN £	MAX £	OPEN
	–	–	47.00	50.00	3-11

H	Westdale Hotel

37 Abbey Road, **HIGHLY COMMENDED**
Llandudno
LL30 2EH
Tel: (01492) 877996

Westdale is a comfortable hotel with a good friendly atmosphere. Situated on the level in a quiet road facing Haulfre Gardens, within easy walking distance of shops and beaches. Large ground and first floor bedrooms with en-suite bathrooms. Centrally heated throughout, choice of menu, licensed bar, car park, dinner optional. S.A.E. for brochure.

P ⚘	SINGLE PER PERSON B&B		DOUBLE FOR 2 PERSONS B&B		🛏12 🛏3
C ♦ ⏢ 🍴	MIN £	MAX £	MIN £	MAX £	OPEN
	16.50	20.00	33.00	40.00	2-11

GH	Dolwen Guest House

7 St Marys Road, **HIGHLY COMMENDED**
Llandudno
LL30 2UB
Tel: (01492) 877757
E-mail: dkyffin@aol.com

Situated within easy reach of shops, beach and North Wales Theatre. Dolwen is a family-run guest house highly recommended by guests. All bedrooms are en-suite with colour TV, clock radio and tea/coffee making facilities. Home comforts with lounge and colour TV. Special diets catered for. Fire certificate. Write or phone for colour brochure.

P ⚘	SINGLE PER PERSON B&B		DOUBLE FOR 2 PERSONS B&B		🛏3 🛏3
⏢ ♦ 🍴	MIN £	MAX £	MIN £	MAX £	OPEN
	–	–	32.00	34.00	3-10

GH	Glenavon Guest House

27 St Marys Road, **HIGHLY COMMENDED**
Llandudno
LL30 2UB
Tel: (01492) 877687

Friendly family-run guest house in garden area of town. Quiet location within few minutes walk to town, beach and all amenities. Golf courses nearby, theatre, dri ski slope. Eight bedrooms, two double and one twin are en-suite. En-suite rooms have TV and tea/coffee facilities. Off street parking. We aim to please.

P ⏢	SINGLE PER PERSON B&B		DOUBLE FOR 2 PERSONS B&B		🛏8 🛏3
♦ 🍴	MIN £	MAX £	MIN £	MAX £	OPEN
	17.00	20.00	32.00	38.00	4-12

GH	Martins Restaurant With Rooms

11 Mostyn Avenue, **HIGHLY COMMENDED**
Craig-y-Don,
Llandudno LL30 1YS
Tel: (01492) 870070
Fax: (01492) 876661

Martins award-winning candlelit restaurant with rooms. Attractive, quality en-suite accommodation to accompany our award winning cuisine. Special breaks available. Close to seafront and theatre. Many celebrities dine and stay at "Martins" and master chef-proprietor Martin James and his partner Jan, look forward to welcoming you.

♦ ⏢	SINGLE PER PERSON B&B		DOUBLE FOR 2 PERSONS B&B		🛏3 🛏3
♦ 🍴	MIN £	MAX £	MIN £	MAX £	OPEN
	–	–	45.00	50.00	1-12

GH	Trevlyn Private Hotel

25 Trinity Avenue, **COMMENDED**
Llandudno
LL30 2SJ
Tel: (01492) 875860

Open 2-10

B&B pp £14.00 - £16.00. Double, B&B £28.00 - £32.00

P ⚘ C ♦ 🍴 ⏢ ♦ 🍴				🛏10 🛏3

GH	Roughsedge Guest House

26/28 Marine Road,  **COMMENDED**
Prestatyn
LL19 7HD
Tel: (01745) 887359
Fax: (01745) 852883

Open 1-11

B&B pp £15.00 - £25.00. Double, B&B £30.00 - £40.00

P C ♦ ⏢ ♦ 🍴				🛏10 🛏3

GH	Sunnyside

146 Dinerth Road, **APPROVED**
Rhos on Sea,
Colwyn Bay
LL28 4YF
Tel: (01492) 544048

A warm welcome at our home just out of Rhos on Sea, adjacent to Colwyn Bay, Llandudno. Ample shopping facilities, close to beaches, golf courses, easy drive to mountains of Snowdonia. Lovely surrounding country views. Good home-cooked breakfast to start off your day. Excellent value accommodation. Welsh speaking.

⏢ ♦	SINGLE PER PERSON B&B		DOUBLE FOR 2 PERSONS B&B		🛏2 🛏1
	MIN £	MAX £	MIN £	MAX £	OPEN
	18.00	18.00	27.00	27.00	3-10

GH	The Links Guest House

20 Beechwood Road, **HIGHLY COMMENDED**
Rhyl LL18 3EU
Tel: (01745) 344381
Fax: (01745) 344381 **GOLD**

Open 1-12

B&B pp £16.00 - £20.00. Double, B&B £28.00 - £32.00

P ⏢ ♦ 🍴				🛏6 🛏5

The North Wales Borderlands

Flint

St Asaph

Denbigh

3

Mold

Ruthin

Wrexham

Llangollen

Wales's border country is mix of rolling green hills, lovely valleys, high moor and forest. The airy Clwydian Range guards the broad and fertile Vale of Clwyd – one of Wales's richest farming areas – which is dotted with historic towns. Llangollen's vale is much deeper, its steep-sided hills rising to dramatic heights in the mountains around the Horseshoe Pass. The wild moorlands above Denbigh are covered in heather and forest – and the waters of Llyn Brenig, a huge reservoir with many leisure facilities. There's much to see and do in this exhilarating area – walking,

riding, canal cruising, and visiting places like Bodelwyddan Castle, where paintings from the National Portrait Gallery are exhibited, and Erddig near Wrexham, an unusual 'upstairs, downstairs' country house owned by the National Trust.

Llangollen Canal

It's a fact...

This area is home to six of the seven 'Wonders of Wales' – Pistyll Rhaeadr Falls, Wrexham Steeple, Overton Yew Trees, Llangollen Bridge and Gresford's Bells. St Winefride's Well, the sixth 'wonder', is visited to this day by pilgrims who come to bathe in its legendary waters. Beatrix Potter found inspiration for her Flopsy Bunnies illustrations at Gwaynynog near Denbigh. The Clwydian Range of hills was designated an 'Area of Outstanding Natural Beauty' in 1985.
St Asaph has Britain's smallest cathedral.

Be7 Corwen

Pleasant market town in Vale of Edeyrnion. Livestock market held regularly. Fishing in River Dee, swimming pool, good walks. Well-located touring centre for Snowdonia and border country.

Be5 Denbigh

Castled town in Vale of Clwyd with much historic interest. Friary and museum. Pony trekking, riding, fishing, golf, tennis and bowls. Gwaynynog Country World farm-based attraction. Indoor heated swimming pool. Centrally located for enjoying the rolling hills of North-east Wales, a rich farming area full of attractive villages.

Cb4 Holywell

Place of pilgrimage for centuries, the 'Lourdes of Wales' with St Winefride's Holy Well. Remains of Basingwerk Abbey (1131) nearby. Leisure centre with swimming pools. Interesting and attractive Greenfield Valley Heritage Park

Be5 Llandyrnog

Village ticked away on the side of the Clwydian Range above the pastoral Vale of Clwyd. Historic Denbigh and Ruthin close by. An excellent walking centre.

Ec1 Llangollen

Romantic town on River Dee, famous for its International Musical Eisteddfod; singers and dancers from all over the world come here every July. The town's many attractions include museums, pottery, weavers, ECTARC European Centre for Traditional and Regional Cultures and a standard-gauge steam railway. Plas Newydd (home of 'Ladies of Llangollen' fame) is nearby. Valle Crucis Abbey is 2 miles away in a superb setting and ruined Castell Dinas Brân overlooks the town. Browse through the town's little shops; stand on its 14th-century stone bridge; cruise along the canal. Golf course and wonderful walking in surrounding countryside.

Cb5 Mold

Town located on edge of the lovely Clwydian Range of hills. Excellent Theatr Clwyd offers wide range of entertainment. Visit Daniel Owen Centre, memorial to the 'Dickens of Wales'. Golf course. Loggerheads Country Park in wooded setting to the west. Good touring centre for country and coast.

Ca6 Ruthin

Attractive and historic market town noted for its fine architecture. Many captivating old buildings. Medieval banquets in Ruthin Castle. Ancient St Peter's Church has beautiful gates and carved panels. Good range of small shops; craft centre with workshops. Ideal base for exploring lovely Vale of Clwyd and Clwydian Range.

Be4 St Asaph

Tiny city with the smallest cathedral in Britain, scene of the annual North Wales Music Festival. Prehistoric Cefn Caves nearby. Pleasantly situated on River Elwy in verdant Vale of Clwyd. Three important historic sites on doorstep - medieval Rhuddlan Castle, Bodelwyddan Castle (with noted art collection) and Bodrhyddan Hall.

Ruthin

H | Corwen Court Private Hotel

London Road,
Corwen
LL21 0DP
Tel: (01490) 412854

 COMMENDED

Situated on the A5. Converted old police station and courthouse. Six prisoners cells now single bedrooms, hand basin in each, three only share two bathrooms. Double bedrooms have en-suite facilities. Comfortable lounge, colour TV. Dining room with separate tables where magistrates once presided. Centrally heated. Fire certificate. Convenient base for touring North Wales.

		SINGLE PER PERSON B&B		DOUBLE FOR 2 PERSONS B&B		🛏 10 🛏 4
		MIN £	MAX £	MIN £	MAX £	OPEN
		14.00	15.00	30.00	32.00	3-11

GH | Cayo Guest House

74 Vale Street,
Denbigh
LL16 3BW
Tel: (01745) 812686

 COMMENDED

Long established centrally situated guest house, ideal base for touring North Wales. Excellent area for walking, golf, gliding and the town has a leisure centre. Good food using local produce, special diets catered for. Well behaved dogs and children welcome. Pick up service for 'Offas Dykers'. AAQQ.

		SINGLE PER PERSON B&B		DOUBLE FOR 2 PERSONS B&B		🛏 6 🛏 4
		MIN £	MAX £	MIN £	MAX £	OPEN
		17.00	17.00	34.00	34.00	1-12

GH | The Grange

Grange Road,
Llangollen
LL20 8AP
Tel: (01978) 860366

 HIGHLY COMMENDED

Attractive country house of character situated in town within a tranquil and secluded 2 acre garden. Pretty en-suite bedrooms, spacious and comfortable with tea/coffee facilities. Family room, twin and double available. Child reductions. Interesting beamed lounge with TV. Safe parking in grounds. 10 minutes walk from centre of Llangollen.

		SINGLE PER PERSON B&B		DOUBLE FOR 2 PERSONS B&B		🛏 3 🛏
		MIN £	MAX £	MIN £	MAX £	OPEN
		25.00	25.00	40.00	40.00	1-12

GH | Pen-y-Bont Fawr

Cynwyd,
Corwen
LL21 0ET
Tel: (01490) 412663

 COMMENDED

Pen-y-Bont Fawr is on the outskirts of Cynwyd Village, near Corwen. Llangollen, Bala, Betws-y-Coed and Snowdonia are all nearby. An ideal area for walking, cycling, fishing and watersports in Bala. Horseriding can be arranged. You can be assured of the legendary Welsh hospitality. Choice of twin or double bedrooms.

		SINGLE PER PERSON B&B		DOUBLE FOR 2 PERSONS B&B		🛏 3 🛏 0
		MIN £	MAX £	MIN £	MAX £	OPEN
C		14.00	16.00	25.00	30.00	1-12

GH | Bryn Beuno Guest House

Whitford Street,
Holywell
CH8 7NJ
Tel: (01352) 711315

 HIGHLY COMMENDED

Highly recommended residence overlooking the Greenfield Valley. Ideal for all seasons for exploring North Wales and its many attractions. Also the beautiful walled city of Chester. First class hospitality and comfort assured with homely atmosphere. Our success is built on the continuation of guests returning and informing others. Brochure available on request.

		SINGLE PER PERSON B&B		DOUBLE FOR 2 PERSONS B&B		🛏 4 🛏
		MIN £	MAX £	MIN £	MAX £	OPEN
		15.00	15.00	28.00	28.00	1-12

GH | Hillcrest Guest House

Hill Street,
Llangollen
LL20 8EU
Tel: (01978) 860208
Fax: (01978) 860208

 HIGHLY COMMENDED
GOLD

This friendly little guest house lies in a quiet area of the town. Pretty bedrooms have fully tiled en-suite shower rooms and all are equipped with TV's and full central heating, one is situated on the ground floor. Wales Welcome Host winner 1996. Fire certificate. AAQQQ Recommended. Car parking in our own grounds.

		SINGLE PER PERSON B&B		DOUBLE FOR 2 PERSONS B&B		🛏 7 🛏 7
		MIN £	MAX £	MIN £	MAX £	OPEN
		-	-	40.00	42.00	1-12

GH | Tyn-Llidiart House

Corwen
LL21 9RS
Tel: (01490) 412727
Fax: (01490) 412729

HIGHLY COMMENDED

A country house set in Dee Valley by river Dee overlooking Berwyn mountains. Corwen is an ideal base for exploring North Wales countryside and coast. En-suite rooms with colour TV, tea/coffee making facilities, hairdryers, shampoo and bathroom aids. Tastefully decorated with pleasant surroundings and a very warm welcome.

		SINGLE PER PERSON B&B		DOUBLE FOR 2 PERSONS B&B		🛏 2 🛏 2
		MIN £	MAX £	MIN £	MAX £	OPEN
		17.00	17.00	34.00	34.00	1-12

GH | Mangetout

Hen Dy'r Esgob
Llandyrnog
LL16 4LT
Tel: (01842) 790526

 HIGHLY COMMENDED
GOLD

Open 1-12

B&B pp £20.00 - £25.00. Double, B&B £40.00 - £50.00

P	C			🛏 3 🛏 -

GH | Bryant Rose

31 Regent Street,
Llangollen LL20 8HN
Tel: (01978) 860389

COMMENDED

Open 4-12

B&B pp Max £17.50. Double, B&B £28.00 - £30.00

P			🛏 3 🛏 -

GH | The Old Vicarage Guest House

Bryn Howel Lane,
Llangollen
LL20 7YR
Tel: (01978) 823018
Fax: (01978) 823018

 HIGHLY COMMENDED

The Old Vicarage is a large, attractive Georgian country residence set in prize winning gardens with a natural stream offering spacious quality accommodation in an exclusive location. Bar meals are available within easy walking distance at the picturesque Canal Marina. From Llangollen take A539 turn at Bryn Howel Hotel. One mile along lane by river.

		SINGLE PER PERSON B&B		DOUBLE FOR 2 PERSONS B&B		🛏 3 🛏 3
		MIN £	MAX £	MIN £	MAX £	OPEN
		-	-	34.00	40.00	1-12

Llangollen Mold Ruthin St Asaph

FGH | Tyn Celyn Farmhouse

Tyndwr,
Llangollen
LL20 8AR
Tel: (01978) 861117

COMMENDED

Spacious oak beamed comfortable farmhouse on the outskirts of Llangollen. Situated in a peaceful valley with wonderful views. All bedrooms have bathrooms en-suite, beverage tray, television and central heating. Ideally situated for all local amenities and for visiting Chester, Snowdonia area and the North Wales coast. One and half miles from town centre. Ample secure parking.

		SINGLE PER PERSON B&B		DOUBLE FOR 2 PERSONS B&B		3
P						3
		MIN £	MAX £	MIN £	MAX £	OPEN
		-	-	37.00	39.00	1-12

GH | Brookside House

Brookside Lane,
Northop Hall
CH7 6HN
Tel: (01244) 821146

HIGHLY COMMENDED

GOLD

Open 1-12

B&B pp £22.00 - £24.00. Double, B&B £32.00 - £38.00

P | 3 | 1

GH | Rhos-y-Gadfa

4 Paddock Way,
Ruthin Road,
Gwernymynydd
Nr Mold CH7 5LA
Tel: (01352) 752339

COMMENDED

Open 1-12

B&B pp Min £20.00 Double, B&B Min £33.00

P | 3 | 3

FH | Maes Garmon Farm

Off Gwernaffield Road,
Gwernaffield,
Mold CH7 5DB
Tel: (01352) 759887

HIGHLY COMMENDED

GOLD

Imagine a peaceful secluded valley, a converted stable adjoining a 17th century farmhouse. A welcome of tea and scones. Accommodation of the highest standard, a wealth of beams, antiques, oak and pine furnishings. Guest lounge, en-suite bedrooms, two double and one twin. Beautiful 3 acre gardens, summerhouse, pond and stream. Convenient for Snowdonia and Chester.

		SINGLE PER PERSON B&B		DOUBLE FOR 2 PERSONS B&B		3
P						3
		MIN £	MAX £	MIN £	MAX £	OPEN
		20.00	24.00	32.00	38.00	1-12

GH | Firgrove

Llanfwrog,
Ruthin
LL15 2LL
Tel: (01824) 702677

HIGHLY COMMENDED

Open 3-11

Double, B&B Min £38.00

P | 3 | 1

GH | The Old Rectory

Clocaenog,
Ruthin LL15 2AT
Tel: (01824) 750740
Fax: (01824) 750740

HIGHLY COMMENDED

Share our spacious Georgian home in peaceful countryside, just 10 minutes from Ruthin, while exploring the many and varied places of interest in Snowdonia, Llangollen or Chester. Return to a comfortable centrally heated house with four bedrooms, 1 family en-suite, or with adjacent bathroom. Relax in your lounge with colour TV, radio and library. Evening meal by prior arrangement.

		SINGLE PER PERSON B&B		DOUBLE FOR 2 PERSONS B&B		4
P	C					2
		MIN £	MAX £	MIN £	MAX £	OPEN
		16.00	18.00	32.00	36.00	1-12

FGH | Plas Uchaf

Graigadwywynt,
Llanfair Dyffryn Clwyd,
Ruthin LL15 2TF
Tel: (01824) 705794

HIGHLY COMMENDED

16th century manor house of historical interest, set in beautiful countryside. Wealth of beams, panelling and log fires. Tastefully decorated and furnished. All rooms with en-suite facilities, TV and tea making facilities. Centrally situated for Snowdonia, Llangollen and Chester. A warm welcome is assured with a Welsh speaking family.

		SINGLE PER PERSON B&B		DOUBLE FOR 2 PERSONS B&B		3
P						3
		MIN £	MAX £	MIN £	MAX £	OPEN
		-	20.00	-	34.00	1-12

FGH | Pant Glas Canol Farm

Bont Uchel,
Ruthin
LL15 2BS
Tel: (01824) 710241/710639

HIGHLY COMMENDED

North Wales 15th century farmhouse bed and breakfast, good food and a warm welcome awaits you. Situated one mile form the A525 and three miles from the medieval town of Ruthin, with pleasant walks and delightful views of the vale of Clwyd.

		SINGLE PER PERSON B&B		DOUBLE FOR 2 PERSONS B&B		3
P						1
		MIN £	MAX £	MIN £	MAX £	OPEN
		15.00	16.00	30.00	32.00	4-12

FH | Llainwen Ucha

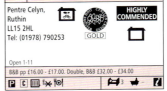

Pentre Celyn,
Ruthin
LL15 2HL
Tel: (01978) 790253

HIGHLY COMMENDED

GOLD

Open 1-11

B&B pp £16.00 - £17.00. Double, B&B £32.00 - £34.00

P | C | | 3 | -

FGH | Plas Penucha

Caerwys,
Mold
CH7 5BH
Tel: (01352) 720210

HIGHLY COMMENDED

GOLD

Welcome to this 16th century farmhouse, altered over succeeding generations but retaining history and serenity in comfortable surroundings. Extensive gardens overlooking Clwydian Hills. Spacious lounge with extensive library. Four well equipped bedrooms, two en-suite. Full central heating, log fires. Two miles from A55 expressway. Ideal touring centre for North Wales and Chester. Brochure from Nest Price.

		SINGLE PER PERSON B&B		DOUBLE FOR 2 PERSONS B&B		4
P						2
		MIN £	MAX £	MIN £	MAX £	OPEN
		18.50	18.50	37.00	37.00	1-12

WALES CYMRU
TWO HOURS AND A MILLION MILES AWAY

Snowdonia
Mountains and Coast

Bangor
Caernarfon
Betws-y-Coed
Blaenau Ffestiniog
Criccieth
Porthmadog
Bala
Pwllheli
Harlech
Barmouth
Dolgellau
Tywyn
Aberdovey

1
2
3
4

This part of Wales takes its name from the jagged pinnacle of Snowdon. Yet the Snowdonia National Park extends southwards for hundreds of square miles from Snowdon itself, all the way to Dolgellau and beyond, and eastwards to Bala. All of Wales's high and mighty mountains are here – Tryfan, the Glyders, the Carneddau, the Aran and Arennigs, and Cader Idris. Snowdonia, a place of surprising scenic variety, also has its oakwood vales, its forested hills, its lakes and rivers, its brooding moorlands. Mountains sweep down to the sea along a beautiful coastline of sandy beaches and estuaries. And along the Llŷn Peninsula – 'Snowdonia's arm' – you'll find some of the wildest coastal scenery in Britain as well as sheltered beaches and picturesque little resorts.

Bala Lake

It's a fact...

The Snowdonia National Park covers 838 square miles. It was Wales's first national park, designated in 1951. Snowdonia's Welsh name is Eryri, which means 'the mountain of the eagles'. The peak of Snowdon stands at 1085m/3560ft, the highest mountain in England and Wales. The Llŷn Peninsula has the highest percentage of Welsh speakers in Wales (75%). Llŷn was declared an 'Area of Outstanding Natural Beauty' in 1956. Bwlch y Groes, the mountain road between Dinas Mawddwy and Bala, is Wales's highest road, climbing to 546m/1791ft. Bala Lake is Wales's largest natural lake.

Db6   Aberdyfi/Aberdovey

Picturesque little resort and dinghy sailor's paradise on the Dovey Estuary. All watersports, thriving yacht club, good inns looking out over the bay and 18-hole golf links. Superb views towards hills and mountains.

Ac5   Abersoch

Resort, dinghy sailing and windsurfing centre with sandy beaches. Superb coastal scenery with easy walks. Pony trekking, golf, fishing and sea trips. Llanengan's historic church nearby.

De2   Bala

Traditional Welsh country town with tree-lined main street and interesting little shops. Narrow-gauge railway runs one side of Bala Lake, 4 miles long (the largest natural lake in Wales) and ringed with mountains. Golf, sailing, fishing, canoeing - and a natural touring centre for Snowdonia.

Ae3   Bangor

Compact cathedral city of character overlooking the Menai Strait; gateway to Anglesey and Snowdonia's Ogwen Valley, with university college and 6th-century cathedral. Attractions include Theatr Gwynedd, Penrhyn Castle, museum and art gallery and an exquisitely renovated pier. Heated swimming pool, yachting and fishing.

Db4   Barmouth

Superbly located resort at the mouth of lovely Mawddach Estuary. Golden sands, miles of wonderful mountain and estuary walks nearby. Promenade, funfair, harbour and pony rides on the beach. Lifeboat and shipwreck museums. Good shops and inns. Excellent parking on seafront.

Ae6   Beddgelert

One of Snowdonia's loveliest mountain villages, home of the legend of Gelert, set amongst glorious scenery - Nant Gwynant Valley to the east and picturesque Aberglaslyn Pass to the south. Winner of numerous awards including Europe in Bloom and Wales in Bloom. Marvellous walks; Wordsworth made a famous dawn ascent of Snowdon from here. Ideal destination for that mountain break. Visit Sygun Copper Mine, a nearby attraction.

Ad5   Betws Garmon

Village between Beddgelert and Caernarfon on north-western approach to Snowdonia range. Rugged, spectacular mountain scenery all around. Close to lake of Llyn Cwellyn. Good walking base.

Bb6   Betws-y-Coed

Wooded village and popular mountain resort in picturesque setting where three rivers meet. Good touring centre, close to best mountain area of Snowdonia. Tumbling rivers and waterfalls emerge from a tangle of treetops. Trout fishing, craft shops, golf course, railway and motor museums, Snowdonia National Park Visitor Centre. Nature trails very popular with hikers. Swallow Falls a 'must'.

Ba7   Blaenau Ffestiniog

One-time centre of the Welsh slate industry, now attracts visitors who come to see two cavernous slate quarries - Llechwedd and Gloddfa Ganol - open to the public. Narrow-gauge Ffestiniog Railway runs from Porthmadog. Nearby Stwlan Dam, part of hydro-electric scheme, reached through marvellous mountain scenery. Visitor centre explains how electricity is generated.

Ad4 Caernarfon

Dominated by magnificent 13th-century castle, most famous of Wales's medieval fortresses. Many museums in castle, maritime museum in town. Narrow-gauge Welsh Highland Railway/Rheilffordd Eryri runs into hills from quay. Caernarfon Air World at Dinas Dinlle, Segontium Roman Fort and Museum on hill above town. Popular sailing centre, old harbour, market square, Lloyd George statue. Holiday centre at gateway of Snowdonia. Parc Glynllifon nearby.

Ba6 Capel Curig

Village ringed by Snowdonia's highest mountains. Great favourite with climbers. Good walking and fishing. Craft shops.

Bb4 Conwy

Historic town with mighty castle and complete ring of medieval town walls. Dramatic estuary setting. Many ancient buildings including Aberconwy House. Telford Suspension Bridge, popular fish quay, spectacular wall walks. Golf, pony trekking, Butterfly House, art gallery, aquarium, pleasure cruises. Tiny 'smallest house' on quay. Touring centre for Snowdonia.

Dc5 Corris

Village in the foothills of Cader Idris mountain range. Excellent craft centre and exciting King Arthur's Labyrinth attraction. Small railway museum. Centre for Alternative Technology, the 'village of the future', close by.

Ad7 Criccieth

Ideal family resort with good beach. Romantic ruined castle on headland overlooking sea. Salmon and trout in nearby rivers and lakes. Festival of Music and the Arts in June. Village of Llanystumdwy with Lloyd George Museum nearby.

Dd4 Dinas Mawddwy

Mountain village famed for its salmon and trout fishing and marvellous walks. On fringes of Snowdonia National Park. Visit the craft and tea shop at the old woollen mill. Drive over the highest road in Wales, the spectacular Bwlch y Groes mountain pass, to Bala.

Dc4 Dolgellau

Handsome stone-built market town which seems to have grown naturally out of the mountains. The heights of Cader Idris loom above the rooftops. Interesting shops, pubs, cafés. Museum of the Quakers in town centre. Visit a gold mine in nearby forest. Excellent base for touring the coast and countryside.

Da3 Dyffryn Ardudwy

Pleasant village near the coast on Barmouth-Harlech road, set between sea and mountains. Prehistoric burial chamber and stone circles nearby; also scenic Shell Island and Museum and Bird Gardens.

Db4 Fairbourne

Quiet resort with 2 miles of sand south of Mawddach Estuary. Railway buffs travel far to ride on its 1'3" gauge Fairbourne and Barmouth Steam Railway.

Db1 Ffestiniog

Stands on a high bluff looking towards the sea. Neighbour of Blaenau Ffestiniog with its slate caverns and narrow-gauge railway. Cynfal Waterfalls spring from the moors above the town.

Da2 Harlech

Small, stone-built town dominated by remains of 13th-century castle - site of Owain Glyndwr's last stand. Dramatically set on a high crag, the castle commands a magnificent panorama of rolling sand dunes, sea and mountains. Home of the 18-hole Royal St David's Golf Club. Shell Island nearby. Theatre and swimming pool. Visitors can explore the chambers of the Chwarel Hên Slate Caverns just south of Harlech.

Ae4 Llanberis

Popular centre for walkers and climbers, least difficult (5 miles) walk to Snowdon summit starts here. For easy ride up take Snowdon Mountain Railway. Many things to see and do in this lively mountain town - Llanberis Lake Railway, slate industry museum, unforgettable trip into the awesome tunnels of the Dinorwig Hydro-Electric Scheme, activity-packed Padarn Country Park, ancient Dolbadarn Castle, Bryn Brâs Castle at nearby Llanrug.

Dc5 Machynlleth

Historic market town near beautiful Dovey Estuary. Owain Glyndwr's Parliament House in the wide handsome main street is now a museum and brass rubbing centre. Superbly equipped Bro Ddyfi Leisure Centre offers wide range of activities. Celtica centre tells the story of Celtic myth and legend. Ancient and modern meet here; the inventive Centre for Alternative Technology is 3 miles away, just off the A487 to Dolgellau. Felin Crewi Flour Mill is off the A489 2 miles to the east.

Ae7 Porthmadog

Harbour town and shopping centre named after William Madocks, who built mile-long Cob embankment. Steam narrow-gauge Ffestiniog Railway runs to Blaenau Ffestiniog, with its slate caverns. Also Welsh Highland Railway. Pottery, maritime museum, car museum. Portmeirion Italianate village and good beaches nearby.

Ac7 Pwllheli

A small resort big in appeal to sailors; many craft are moored in its attractive marina. Promenade with excellent spacious beach, shopping, golf, leisure centre. River and sea fishing. Exciting Starcoast World, a major North Wales attraction, nearby.

Dc5 Tal-y-llyn

Lakeside village in magnificent setting below Cader Idris mountain, ideally placed for fishing and walking. Narrow-gauge Talyllyn Railway, which runs to a nearby halt, connects with Tywyn.

Bb5 Trefriw

Woollen mill village on western side of Conwy Valley, with Trefriw Wells Spa. Lakes at Llyn Geirionydd and Llyn Crafnant, both local beauty spots. Good walking country.

Da6 Tywyn

Seaside resort on Cardigan Bay, with beach activities, sea and river fishing and golf among its leading attractions. Good leisure centre. Narrow-gauge Talyllyn Railway runs inland from here and St Cadfan's Stone and Llanegryn Church are important Christian monuments. In the hills stand Castell-y-Bere, a native Welsh castle, and Bird Rock, a haven for birdlife.

Harlech

FGH | Tyddyn Rhys Farm

Aberdovey
LL35 0PG
Tel: (01654) 767533

HIGHLY COMMENDED

A quiet comfortable farmhouse with homely atmosphere. Panoramic view of Cardigan Bay with picturesque walks in area. One en-suite, one double and one single bedroom with tea/coffee making facilities, colour TV in all bedrooms. Championship golf course, tennis and bowls within one mile. A warm welcome awaits you at Tyddyn Rhys.

P	🛏	SINGLE PER PERSON		DOUBLE FOR 2 PERSONS B&B		🛏 3
✻		MIN £	MAX £	MIN £	MAX £	OPEN
		–	20.00	–	38.00	3-11

GH | Llysfor Guest House

Abersoch
Pwllheli
LL53 7AL
Tel: (01758) 712248

COMMENDED

A well established family-run guest house, our aim is to please and make your stay enjoyable. Hot and cold water, shaver points, tea/coffee facilities in all bedrooms. Some en-suite rooms. Comfortable dining room, separate lounge with TV. One minute to beach overlooking harbour. Private parking, own grounds. Fire Certificate. Reduced rates for children. Enquiries Mr Hiorns. ℹ

P	🐕	SINGLE PER PERSON B&B		DOUBLE FOR 2 PERSONS B&B		🛏 7
♨		MIN £	MAX £	MIN £	MAX £	OPEN
		16.00	17.00	34.00	40.00	4-10

GH | Frondderw Private Hotel

Stryd-y-Fron
Bala
LL23 7YD
Tel: (01678) 520301

COMMENDED | GOLD

Charming period mansion quietly situated on hillside overlooking Bala town and lake. All rooms have comfortable beds, hot/cold water, central heating, tea/coffee making facilities. Lounge, free parking. Home cooking, dinner optional, vegetarian/special diets on request. Licensed. Ideal centre for touring, walking and water sports. Concessionary golf. ℹ

P	♨	SINGLE PER PERSON B&B		DOUBLE FOR 2 PERSONS B&B		🛏 8
🍴		MIN £	MAX £	MIN £	MAX £	OPEN
		16.00	22.00	32.00	44.00	3-11

GH | Bronwylfa Guest House

LLandderfel,
Bala
LL23 7HG
Tel: (01678) 530207
Fax: (01678) 530207

DE LUXE AWARD

Victorian country house, private gardens, large car parking. Central for touring Snowdonia National Park, beautiful views Berwyn Mountains. Large en-suite rooms, victorian conservatory. Home from home friendly peaceful and relaxing atmosphere with home-cooking. Village Inn with restaurant, short walk away over River Dee, 4 miles Bala, 6 miles from A5 west 4 miles south towards Bala. Non-smoking.

P	🐕	SINGLE PER PERSON B&B		DOUBLE FOR 2 PERSONS B&B		🛏 3
C	♨	MIN £	MAX £	MIN £	MAX £	OPEN
✻ 🍴		25.00	25.00	37.00	44.00	1-12

GH | Plas Gower

Llangower,
Bala
LL23 7BY
Tel: (01678) 520431
Fax: (01678) 520431

HIGHLY COMMENDED

Welcoming Georgian stone house with beautiful views over Bala Lake and surrounding mountains. The lakeshore is only two minutes walk away. Peaceful, relaxed atmosphere, log fires, lovely garden. Ideal for walking, sailing or exploring the delights of Mid and North Wales. Many eating places in Bala, two and a half miles away. ℹ

P	🛏	SINGLE PER PERSON B&B		DOUBLE FOR 2 PERSONS B&B		🛏 2
C	✻	MIN £	MAX £	MIN £	MAX £	OPEN
		18.50	19.50	37.00	39.00	1-12

GH | Trem-y-Wawr

Cae Groes,
Bala
LL23 7AQ
Tel: (01678) 520994

COMMENDED

Private house in an elevated position in countryside with a view of Bala town and lake. Five minutes walk to leisure centre, lake, town and restaurants. Modern rooms with central heating, radio/alarms, TV, tea and coffee tray. Lovely garden. Ideal centre for touring. A range of of outdoor activities including water sports nearby. Full Welsh breakfast. ℹ

P	🛏	SINGLE PER PERSON B&B		DOUBLE FOR 2 PERSONS B&B		🛏 3
✻		MIN £	MAX £	MIN £	MAX £	OPEN
		16.00	20.00	32.00	40.00	3-10

FGH | Erw Feurig Farm Guest House

Cefnddwysarn,
Nr Bala
LL23 7LL
Tel: (01678) 530262
Fax: (01678) 530262

HIGHLY COMMENDED

Open 1-12

B&B pp £15.00 - £20.00. Double, B&B £30.00 - £36.00

P	🛏					🛏 4 🛏 3

FH | Tŷ Gwyn Bungalow

Rhyduchaf,
Bala
LL23 7BD
Tel: (01678) 521267

AWAITING GRADING

Open 4-10

B&B pp £16.00 Double, B&B £28.00 - £32.00

P	🐕	C	🛏	✻	🍴	🛏 2 🛏 – ℹ

GH | Nant y Fedw

Tre Felin,
Llandegai, Bangor
LL57 4LH
Tel: (01248) 351683

HIGHLY COMMENDED

Delightful 150 year old cottage situated in countryside near Penrhyn Castle between Snowdonia mountains and the sea. It has a wealth of charms enhanced by original beams, open fires, antique furnishings and a restful sitting room for guests. All rooms have tea and coffee facilities, radio alarm clocks, hairdryers, colour TV, door and room keys. AA QQQQ Select. ℹ

P	🐕	SINGLE PER PERSON B&B		DOUBLE FOR 2 PERSONS B&B		🛏 2
🛏 ♨		MIN £	MAX £	MIN £	MAX £	OPEN
		23.00	25.00	36.00	36.00	1-12

FH | Goetre Isaf Farmhouse

Caernarfon Road,
Bangor
LL57 4DB
Tel: (01248) 364541
Fax: (01248) 364541

COMMENDED

Open 1-12

B&B pp Min £15.50 - £25.00. Double, B&B £27.00 - £37.00

P	🐕	🛏	♨	🍴	🛏 3 🛏 1 ℹ

GH | Endeavour Guest House

Marine Parade,
Barmouth
LL42 1NA
Tel: (01341) 280271

APPROVED

Open 1-12

B&B pp £16.00 - £18.50. Double, B&B £32.00 - £37.00

🛏	🍴	🛏 9 🛏 5 ℹ

Barmouth Beddgelert Betws Garmon Betws-y-Coed

GH | Fronoleu Hall Guest House

Llanaber,
Barmouth
LL42 1YT
Tel: (01341) 280491
Fax: (01341) 280491

COMMENDED

GOLD

Open 3-10

B&B pp £18.00 - £22.00. Double, B&B £30.00 - £40.00

GH | The Sandpiper

7 Marine Parade,
Barmouth
LL42 1NA
Tel: (01341) 280318

HIGHLY COMMENDED

Situated on Barmouth seafront, The Sandpiper is owned by Susan and John Palmer who, as keen walkers can offer local advice. There is parking outside and the station is a short, level walk. Most double rooms have en-suite facilities including a ground floor bedroom. All rooms have television and free tea/coffee. No pets.

	SINGLE PER PERSON B&B		DOUBLE FOR 2 PERSONS B&B		11 / 6
	MIN £	MAX £	MIN £	MAX £	OPEN
	14.50	15.50	27.00	36.00	3-10

GH | Ael y Bryn

Caernarfon Road,
Beddgelert LL55 4UY
Tel: (01766) 890310
Fax: (01766) 890629
E-mail: ay.b@email.wales.com
Internet: www.nwi.co.uk/aelybryn

COMMENDED

Open 1-12

B&B Double £33.00 - £40.00

GH | Colwyn

Beddgelert
LL55 4UY
Tel: (01766) 890276

COMMENDED

Small riverside cottage guest house c1700. Beamed lounge. En-suite bedrooms, fresh white linen. Warm comfortable and friendly. In the centre of a pretty village right at the foot of Snowdon. Wooded mountains lakes and streams. At the heart of the National Park. With little village shops, inns and cafes. Booking usually essential. B&B £16-£19. Walkers (muddy boots) and wet dogs welcome. Also tiny cottage sleeps two £165 per week.

	SINGLE PER PERSON B&B		DOUBLE FOR 2 PERSONS B&B		3 / 3
	MIN £	MAX £	MIN £	MAX £	OPEN
	16.00	–	–	–	1-12

FH | Hafod y Wern

Betws Garmon,
Caernarfon
LL54 7AQ
Tel: (01286) 650670

HIGHLY COMMENDED

Situated in a beautiful valley at the foot of Mynedd Mawr. Many public footpaths lead from the house through the hamlet of Betws Garmon. The beaches of Anglesey and Caernarfon are within easy reach. Horse riding is also available in nearby Waunfawr. The comfortable bedrooms have tea/coffee facilities, colour TV and central heating.

		SINGLE PER PERSON B&B		DOUBLE FOR 2 PERSONS B&B		3 / –
		MIN £	MAX £	MIN £	MAX £	OPEN
		16.00	16.00	32.00	32.00	1-12

H | Cross Keys Hotel & Restaurant

Betws-y-Coed
LL2 0BN
Tel: (01690) 710334

COMMENDED

Open 1-12

B&B pp £20.00 - £25.00. Double, B&B £37.00 - £43.00

14 / 14

H | Fairy Glen Hotel

Dolwyddelan Road,
Betws-y-Coed
LL24 0SH
Tel: (01690) 710269
Fax: (01690) 710269

HIGHLY COMMENDED

A warm and friendly welcome awaits you at our 17th century family run hotel overlooking the River Conwy amongst mountains and forests. All rooms centrally heated, radio, colour TV, beverage tray. Choice of menu for evening cooked evening meal and traditional Welsh breakfasts. Private parking. Residential licence. Colour brochure available. AA/RAC.

	SINGLE PER PERSON B&B		DOUBLE FOR 2 PERSONS B&B		8 / 6
	MIN £	MAX £	MIN £	MAX £	OPEN
	20.00	23.00	41.00	45.00	2-11

Beddgelert

H | Swallow Falls Hotel

Betws-y-Coed
LL24 0DW
Tel: (01690) 710796
Fax: (01690) 710191

COMMENDED

Situated just outside the picturesque village of Betws-y-Coed opposite Wales most beautiful waterfall, nestling between majestic mountains, streams and rivers. Superb for walkers, climbers or an ideal stopover. Charming pub and licensed tavern bar offering delicious home cooked food. Extensive landscaped gardens with play area. Best value for money hotel in the area.

		SINGLE PER PERSON B&B		DOUBLE FOR 2 PERSONS B&B		🛏11 🛏11
		MIN £	MAX £	MIN £	MAX £	OPEN
		-	-	35.00	50.00	1-12

GH | Aberconwy House

Llanrwst Road,
Betws-y-Coed
LL24 0HD
Tel: (01690) 710202
Fax: (01690) 710800
E-mail: clive-muskus@celtic.co.uk

HIGHLY COMMENDED

Aberconwy House is situated in a quiet position overlooking the popular and picturesque village. It is superbly and tastefully refurnished with all facilities for comfort and relaxation. Beautiful views of the Llugwy Valley, surrounding mountains and the Conwy and Llugwy rivers. Robust breakfast and warm welcome awaiting Ann and Clive Muskus.

		SINGLE PER PERSON B&B		DOUBLE FOR 2 PERSONS B&B		🛏8 🛏8
		MIN £	MAX £	MIN £	MAX £	OPEN
		-	-	44.00	48.00	1-12

GH | Bron Celyn Guest House

Lôn Muriau
Llanrwst Road,
Betws-y-Coed LL24 0HD
Tel: (01690) 710333
Fax: (01690) 710111

HIGHLY COMMENDED

GOLD

Enjoy traditional comfort and home cooking in a relaxed atmosphere. Situated within the Snowdonia National Park overlooking pituresque village of Betws-y-Coed. We provide the ideal base for exploring this interesting area. Most rooms en-suite with a delightful cottage annexe. Hearty breakfast, packed lunches, snacks, evening meals, excellent choice for vegetarians. Special diets catered for by arrangement.

		SINGLE PER PERSON B&B		DOUBLE FOR 2 PERSONS B&B		🛏5 🛏4
		MIN £	MAX £	MIN £	MAX £	OPEN
		22.00	25.00	38.00	46.00	1-12

GH | Bryn Afon Guest House

Pentre Felin
Betws-y-Coed
LL24 0BB
Tel: (01690) 710403

HIGHLY COMMENDED

A lovely Victorian stone house overlooking river and Pont-y-Pair Bridge. Warm welcoming home ideal for touring, walking, golfing, fishing and historical sites. TV, beverage tray in all rooms, some en-suite. Hearty breakfast, private parking. Friendly welcome awaits you.

		SINGLE PER PERSON B&B		DOUBLE FOR 2 PERSONS B&B		🛏7 🛏4
		MIN £	MAX £	MIN £	MAX £	OPEN
		18.00	25.00	32.00	40.00	1-12

GH | Bryn Llewelyn

Holyhead Road
Betws-y-Coed
LL24 0BN
Tel: (01690) 710601
Fax: (01690) 710601

COMMENDED

GOLD

Featured in the BBC production 'The Essential English Guide to Britain', this family run Victorian guest house is in an excellent position to explore the Snowdonia National Park. Comfortable rooms are mostly en-suite with central heating, beverage trays and CTV. Ample private parking. AAQQ RAC Recommended. Non-smoking.

		SINGLE PER PERSON B&B		DOUBLE FOR 2 PERSONS B&B		🛏7 🛏4
		MIN £	MAX £	MIN £	MAX £	OPEN
		15.00	20.50	30.00	41.00	1-12

GH | Coed-y-Fron Guest House

Vicarage Road,
Betws-y-Coed
LL24 0BL
Tel: (01690) 710365

COMMENDED

A lovely Victorian house in the middle of village. Enjoys a quiet elevated position with superb outlook over Betws-y-Coed, the premier touring centre of Snowdonia. Dining room, lounge, seven bedrooms, two en-suite plus two extra bathrooms. All have hot/cold water, central heating, tea/coffee, colour TV, parking. Hearty breakfast and a warm welcome awaits you. AAQQ Recommended

		SINGLE PER PERSON B&B		DOUBLE FOR 2 PERSONS B&B		🛏7 🛏2
		MIN £	MAX £	MIN £	MAX £	OPEN
		16.00	18.00	32.00	40.00	1-12

GH | The Ferns Non-Smokers Guest House

Holyhead Road,
Betws-y-Coed
LL24 0AN
Tel: (01690) 710587
Fax: (01690) 710587

HIGHLY COMMENDED

Open 1-12

B&B pp £20.00 - £25.00. Double, B&B £40.00 - £42.00

🅿 🍷 🛏 ☆✖ 🍳 | 🛏9 🛏9 ℹ

GH | Fron Heulog Country House

Betws-y-Coed
LL24 0BL
Tel: (01690) 710736
Fax: (01690) 710736

HIGHLY COMMENDED

GOLD
AWARD

"The country house in the village". Friendly welcome from Jean and Peter Whittingham to their elegant Victorian stone house in peaceful wooded riverside scenery. Ideal Snowdonia centre – tour, walk, relax. Excellent modern accommodation – comfort, warmth, style. Premium bedrooms have full en-suite bathrooms. Recommended by "Which?" More home than hotel!. Croeso! Welcome!

		SINGLE PER PERSON B&B		DOUBLE FOR 2 PERSONS B&B		🛏3 🛏3
		MIN £	MAX £	MIN £	MAX £	OPEN
		-	-	40.00	50.00	1-12

GH | Glan Llugwy Guest House

Holyhead Road,
Betws-y-Coed
LL24 0BN
Tel: (01690) 710592

COMMENDED

A friendly welcome awaits all visitors from Graham and Jean Brayne in this small homely guest house overlooking the River LLugwy and Gwydir Forest. Beautiful walking country with amenities for golf, fishing and touring. All rooms centrally heated, TV, washbasins, tea/coffee making facilities. Guest lounge, private parking, fire certificate held. Croeso.

		SINGLE PER PERSON B&B		DOUBLE FOR 2 PERSONS B&B		🛏5 🛏-
		MIN £	MAX £	MIN £	MAX £	OPEN
		14.00	17.00	28.00	34.00	1-12

Pets Welcome

You'll see from the symbols that many places to stay welcome dogs and pets by prior arrangement. Although some sections of beach may have restrictions, there are always adjacent areas - the promenade, for example, or quieter stretches of sands - where dogs can be exercised on and sometimes off leads. Please ask at a Tourist Information Centre.

Betws-y-Coed Blaenau Ffestiniog Caernarfon

GH   Mairlys Guest House

Holyhead Road,
Betws-y-Coed
LL24 0AN
Tel: (01690) 710190

HIGHLY COMMENDED

Situated close to village centre. Ideal for walking, touring, golfing and fishing. Mairlys is a non-smoking establishment. Full central heating. Double rooms en-suite, colour TV, coffe/tea facilities in all bedrooms.

		SINGLE PER PERSON B&B		DOUBLE FOR 2 PERSONS B&B		OPEN
		MIN £	MAX £	MIN £	MAX £	
		21.00	23.00	40.00	48.00	1-12

Beds: 5 / 3

FH   Fferm Maes Gwyn

Pentrefoelas,
Betws-y-Coed
LL24 0LR
Tel: (01690) 770668

HIGHLY COMMENDED

Maes Gwyn is a 17th century farmhouse with oak beams and panelling. Separate lounge and dining room both have log/coal fires. Situated in lovely quiet contryside six miles from Betws-y-Coed within reach of Snowdonia, coast, slatemines, woollen mills, forest walks etc. Two bedrooms both have tea/coffee facilities and hot/cold water.

		SINGLE PER PERSON B&B		DOUBLE FOR 2 PERSONS B&B		OPEN
		MIN £	MAX £	MIN £	MAX £	
		16.00	17.00	32.00	34.00	4-11

Beds: 2 / -

GH   Afallon

Manod Road,
Blaenau Ffestiniog
LL41 4AE
Tel: (01766) 830468

HIGHLY COMMENDED

Family-run guest house situated in Snowdonia National Park. Good food, clean homely accommodation, washbasin, shaver point, colour TV, tea/coffee facilities, separate shower, bathroom, toilet. Slate mines, narrow gauge railways, sandy beaches, climbing all within easy reach. Children reduced rates. Dogs welcome. A warm Welsh welcome awaits all our guests. Mrs Griffiths.

		SINGLE PER PERSON B&B		DOUBLE FOR 2 PERSONS B&B		OPEN
		MIN £	MAX £	MIN £	MAX £	
		13.50	15.00	27.00	30.00	1-12

Beds: 3 / -

GH   Mount Pleasant

Holyhead Road,
Betws-y-Coed
LL24 0BN
Tel: (01690) 710502

HIGHLY COMMENDED

A warm Welsh welcome awaits you at our Victorian stone built house, a few minutes walk from the centre of Betws-y-Coed. All home comforts provided in our spotlessly clean double rooms with woodland views. Hearty breakfast served at individual tables. Vegetarian diets catered for. No children under 10. Non-smokers only. Phone for brochure.

		SINGLE PER PERSON B&B		DOUBLE FOR 2 PERSONS B&B		OPEN
		MIN £	MAX £	MIN £	MAX £	
		20.00	25.00	30.00	39.00	1-12

Beds: 4 / 2

FH   Royal Oak Farmhouse

Betws-y-Coed
LL24 0AH
Tel: (01690) 710427

HIGHLY COMMENDED

Old water mill situated on lovely meander of river Llugwy. Three minutes walk from village, secluded but not isolated. Beautiful walks all round the area. Fishing from grounds. Golf course adjacent. Ideal touring centre for North Wales and Snowdonia.

		SINGLE PER PERSON B&B		DOUBLE FOR 2 PERSONS B&B		OPEN
		MIN £	MAX £	MIN £	MAX £	
		-	-	32.00	36.00	1-12

Beds: 3 / 2

H   Menai Bank Hotel

North Road,
Caernarfon
LL55 1BD
Tel: (01286) 673297
Fax: (01286) 673297

HIGHLY COMMENDED

Family owned period hotel. Original features. Extensive coastal views. Close castle and Snowdonia. Tastefully decorated, comfortable bedrooms, one ground floor, colour TV, tea makers, clock radios. Attractive restaurant, varied menus, bar, residents lounge, pool table. Car parking, payphone, lawned flower garden, credit cards, colour brochure, AA/RAC**

		SINGLE PER PERSON B&B		DOUBLE FOR 2 PERSONS B&B		OPEN
		MIN £	MAX £	MIN £	MAX £	
		20.00	-	33.00	50.00	1-12

Beds: 15 / 11

GH   Riverside Restaurant

Holyhead Road,
Betws-y-Coed
LL24 0BN
Tel: (01690) 710650
Fax: (01690) 710650
E-mail: river_side@compuserve.com

COMMENDED

Small guest house with award-winning restaurant, close to village centre. All rooms tea tray, colour television. Riverside is completely non-smoking and has residential licence. Small lounge bar. Within walking distance of station and bus stops.

		SINGLE PER PERSON B&B		DOUBLE FOR 2 PERSONS B&B		OPEN
		MIN £	MAX £	MIN £	MAX £	
		13.00	13.00	22.00	26.00	1-12

Beds: 4 / 1

FGH   Tŷ-Coch Farm & Trekking Centre

Penmachno,
Betws-y-Coed
LL25 0HJ
Tel: (01690) 760248

COMMENDED

Open 1-12

B&B pp £17.00 - £19.00. Double, B&B £34.00 - £38.00

Beds: 3 / 3

WALES TOURIST MAP

- Our best selling map - fully updated and improved for 1998
- Detailed 5 miles/inch scale
- Wealth of tourist information
- Specially devised car tours
- Town plans

£2.35 inc. p&p

(see 'Guides and Maps' at the end of the book)

GH   Chatham Farmhouse

LLandwrog,
Caernarfon
LL54 5TG
Tel: (01286) 831257

HIGHLY COMMENDED

Enjoy a warm welcome in our 18th century house close to safe, sandy beach, Foryd Bay nature reserve, noted for its bird life and historic Caernarfon. Ideal for touring Snowdonias many attractions. Pretty en-suite bedrooms with well stocked refreshment trays. Organic vegetables, free range eggs. Pleasant gardens. Peaceful environment.

		SINGLE PER PERSON B&B		DOUBLE FOR 2 PERSONS B&B		OPEN
		MIN £	MAX £	MIN £	MAX £	
		20.00	20.00	36.00	36.00	3-10

Beds: 3 / 2

GH — The White House

Llanfaglan,
Caernarfon
LL54 5RA
Tel: (01286) 673003

  HIGHLY COMMENDED

Large quietly situated country house in own grounds with magnificent views to sea and mountains. All rooms have en-suite or private facilities, colour TV, tea/coffee makers. One bedroom on ground floor. Guests are wecome to use outdoor pool and gardens in summer. Ideal for ornithologists, walkers, golf, visiting Welsh castles and Snowdonia National Park.

P	🐕	SINGLE PER PERSON B&B		DOUBLE FOR 2 PERSONS B&B		🛏 4
C	🛏					🛏 3
♨		MIN £	MAX £	MIN £	MAX £	OPEN
		22.00	24.00	36.00	40.00	3-11

FH — Llwyndu Mawr Farmhouse

Carmel Road,
Penygroes
LL54 6PU
Tel: (01286) 880419

COMMENDED

Snowdonia, Caernarfon six miles. Working sheep farm, guest house, B&B, evening meal optional. En-suite available. Tea/coffee making facilities. TV lounge, homely atmosphere. Secluded gardens. Delightful rural setting yet within walking distance of Penygroes village for shops, pubs. Lovely mountains and sea views, beach four miles. Telephone Mrs Williams. AA listed.

P	🐕	SINGLE PER PERSON B&B		DOUBLE FOR 2 PERSONS B&B		🛏 4
C	🛏					🛏 1
♨	🍴	MIN £	MAX £	MIN £	MAX £	OPEN
		13.00	18.00	26.00	36.00	1-12

GH — Glan Heulog Guest House

Woodlands,
Llanwrst Road,
Conwy
LL32 8LT
Tel: (01492) 593845

  COMMENDED

Close to Conwy Castle and historic old town. Ideal centre for touring Snowdonia, North Wales coast, Bodnant Garden, Anglesey. TV, tea/coffee in all bedrooms. Our guests say 'Great rooms', 'Excellent service', 'Lovely warm welcome', 'Excellent value for money', 'Best place we have stayed in', 'We'll be back'. Quiet location, good views, attractive garden.

P	🍷	SINGLE PER PERSON B&B		DOUBLE FOR 2 PERSONS B&B		🛏 6
🛏	♨					🛏 5
🍴		MIN £	MAX £	MIN £	MAX £	OPEN
		15.00	20.00	26.00	34.00	1-12

FH — Cae'r Efail Farm

Llanfaglan,
Caernarfon
LL54 5RE
Tel: (01286) 676226/672824
Fax: (01286) 676226

DE LUXE

Cae'r Efail enjoys perfect tranquillity and seclusion with splendid views of Snowdonia and Menai Strait. Central base for all attractions of North Wales, Caernarfon with its magnificent castle is only 2 miles and Dinas Dinlle beach 4 miles. Homely and warm welcome assured with plenty of good home-cooking. Bedrooms have excellent views and facilities.

P	🐕	SINGLE PER PERSON B&B		DOUBLE FOR 2 PERSONS B&B		🛏 2
🛏	🍴					🛏 2
♨		MIN £	MAX £	MIN £	MAX £	OPEN
		18.00	20.00	36.00	40.00	4-10

FH — Pengwern

Saron, Llanwnda,
Caernarfon LL54 5UH
Tel: (01286) 831500
Fax: (01286) 831500
Mobile: (0378) 411780
E-mail: jhjgr@enterprise.net

 AWARD DE LUXE GOLD

Charming spacious farmhouse of character, beautifully situated between mountains and sea, unobstructed views of Snowdonia. Well appointed bedrooms, all en-suite. Land runs down to Foryd Bay, noted for its bird life. Jane Rowlands has a cookery diploma and provides excellent meals with farmhouse fresh food using local produce. Excellent access.

P	🛏	SINGLE PER PERSON B&B		DOUBLE FOR 2 PERSONS B&B		🛏 3
✗	🍴					🛏 3
		MIN £	MAX £	MIN £	MAX £	OPEN
		–	–	46.00	50.00	2-11

FH — Waen Newydd

LLanbedr-y-Cennin,
Conwy
LL32 8UR
Tel: (01492) 660527
Fax: (01492) 660155

HIGHLY COMMENDED GOLD

Welcome to our 19th century cottage, spacious grounds high above village with superb views. Twin en-suite bedroom, lounge with wood burning stove, own dining room, fridge, tea/coffee facilties, TV. Packed lunches by prior arrangement. Ideal for walkers and artists, near to Bodnant Garden, Betws-y-Coed, Trefriw and Conwy bird reserve. Excellent touring base. Good value meals locally.

P	🛏	SINGLE PER PERSON B&B		DOUBLE FOR 2 PERSONS B&B		🛏 1
✗						🛏 1
		MIN £	MAX £	MIN £	MAX £	OPEN
		20.00	20.00	40.00	40.00	1-12

FH — Lleuar Fawr

Penygroes,
Caernarfon
LL54 6PB
Tel: (01286) 660268

 HIGHLY COMMENDED

17th century listed farmhouse set in peaceful location central for exploring mountains of Snowdonia, Llyn Peninsula, Isle of Anglesey and historic town of Caernarfon. Farm noted for bird and wild life, salmon and trout fishing. Two spacious en-suite bedrooms with colour TV, tea making facilities. Children at reduced rates. Warm Welsh welcome awaits you.

P	✗	SINGLE PER PERSON B&B		DOUBLE FOR 2 PERSONS B&B		🛏 2
						🛏 2
		MIN £	MAX £	MIN £	MAX £	OPEN
		25.00	25.00	36.00	40.00	1-11

GH — Llugwy Guest House

Capel Curig
Nr Betws-y-Coed
LL24 0ES
Tel: (01690) 720218

 COMMENDED

Established over 100 years, located in centre of village five miles from Snowdon. Ideal for walking, climbing, boating, fishing, beaches, castles, dry ski slope. Two public lounges one with TV, beamed dining room, central heating, tea/coffee facilities in bedrooms. Superb mountain views. Private car park. Friendly advice on local area if required.

P	🐕	SINGLE PER PERSON B&B		DOUBLE FOR 2 PERSONS B&B		🛏 6
🛏	♨					🛏 –
🍴		MIN £	MAX £	MIN £	MAX £	OPEN
		18.00	20.00	30.00	34.00	1-12

H — Braich Goch Hotel

Corris,
SY20 9RD
Tel: (01654) 761229
Fax: (01654) 761229

 COMMENDED

Set in beautiful surroundings in foothills of Snowdonia. Rooms en-suite or private facilities. Bar meals or restaurant. Centre for Alternative Technology, King Arthurs Labyrinth and Celtica Centre all nearby. Beach within easy reach, walking, fishing, golf, horseriding, steam trains all close by. Activity holidays arranged. Pets welcome. Children over 5. Warm welcome assured.

P	🐕	SINGLE PER PERSON B&B		DOUBLE FOR 2 PERSONS B&B		🛏 6
🍷	♨					🛏 4
🍴		MIN £	MAX £	MIN £	MAX £	OPEN
		25.00	–	39.00	–	1-12

Criccieth Dinas Mawddwy Dolgellau

H | Glyn y Coed Hotel

HIGHLY COMMENDED
GOLD

Portmadog Road,
Criccieth LL52 0HL
Tel: (01766) 522870
Fax: (01766) 523341

Beautiful Victorian house overlooking sea, mountains, castles and near Portmeirion. Cosy bar, highly recommended home-cooking catering for most diets. En-suite bedrooms one on ground floor. Private parking. Senior rates. AA/RAC Acclaimed. Les Routiers Michelin Recommended. Most credit cards accepted. Self-catering available sleeping 2-10. Excellent value in superior accommodation ensures perfect holiday. Brochure with pleasure.

P ♞ ♨ 🛏 🍽 C	SINGLE PER PERSON B&B		DOUBLE FOR 2 PERSONS B&B		🛏10 🛏10
	MIN £	MAX £	MIN £	MAX £	OPEN
	20.00	25.00	40.00	50.00	1-12

H | Min y Gaer Hotel

HIGHLY COMMENDED

Porthmadog Road,
Criccieth
LL52 0HP
Tel: (01766) 522151
Fax: (01766) 523540
E-mail: minygaer.hotel@virgin.net

A pleasant licensed hotel, conveniently situated near the beach with delightful views of Criccieth Castle, Cardigan Bay coastline. Ten comfortable, centrally heated rooms, colour TV and tea/coffee making facilities. Non-smoking rooms available. An ideal base for touring Snowdonia and the Llŷn Peninsula. Private car parking. AA Recommended. RAC Acclaimed.

P ♞ C ♨ 🛏 🍽	SINGLE PER PERSON B&B		DOUBLE FOR 2 PERSONS B&B		🛏10 🛏9
	MIN £	MAX £	MIN £	MAX £	OPEN
	19.50	22.50	39.00	45.00	3-10

GH | Y Rhoslyn

COMMENDED

8 Marine Terrace,
Criccieth LL52 0EF
Tel: (01766) 522685
E-mail: pefhay@premier.co.uk

Friendly family-run guest house in unspoilt traditional seaside resort of Criccieth. On the seafront, some rooms with lovely sea and mountain views. Castle and superb ice cream close by. Snowdonia and Llŷn Peninsula easily reached. All rooms with TV, washbasin, tea and coffee facilities. Guest lounge. Families, children welcome.

♨ 🛏 ♦	SINGLE PER PERSON B&B		DOUBLE FOR 2 PERSONS B&B		🛏6 🛏2
	MIN £	MAX £	MIN £	MAX £	OPEN
	14.00	22.50	25.00	35.00	3-10

H | Red Lion Hotel

COMMENDED

Dinas Mawddwy,
Nr Machynlleth
SY20 9JA
Tel: (01650) 531247

Open 1-12

B&B pp £16.50 - £17.50. Double, B&B £36.00 - £40.00

P ♞ ♨ 🛏 🍽 | 🛏5 🛏2 |

FGH | Bryncelyn Farm

HIGHLY COMMENDED
GOLD

Dinas Mawddy,
Machynlleth
SY20 9JG
Tel: (01650) 531289

A warm welcome awaits you at Bryncelyn Farm, located in the peaceful Cywarch Valley at the foot of Aranfawddwy 3000ft with beautiful unspoilt views, an excellent location for walking and climbing. Spacious en-suite bedrooms with tea/coffee making facilities, colour television and heating. Ideal base for touring Mid Wales, Snowdonia and seaside. Five minutes away from the main A470 North to South road.

P ♞ C 🛏 🍽	SINGLE PER PERSON B&B		DOUBLE FOR 2 PERSONS B&B		🛏2 🛏2
	MIN £	MAX £	MIN £	MAX £	OPEN
	20.00	–	36.00	–	1-12

GH | Clifton House Hotel

COMMENDED

Smithfield Square,
Dolgellau
LL40 1ES
Tel: (01341) 422554
Fax: (01341) 423580

Take your scrumptious Welsh breakfast in the former Meirionnydd county gaol. Our historic town house offers the friendly welcome of a bed and breakfast with all the freedom of a hotel. Spacious rooms with all facilities make us an ideal base to explore beautiful southern Snowdonia.

C 🛏 ♨ ♦	SINGLE PER PERSON B&B		DOUBLE FOR 2 PERSONS B&B		🛏6 🛏4
	MIN £	MAX £	MIN £	MAX £	OPEN
	–	25.00	30.00	45.00	1-12

Prices

In this publication we go to great lengths to make sure that you have a clear, accurate idea of prices and facilities. It's all spelled out in the 'Prices' section - and remember to confirm everything when making your booking.

H | Fronoleu Farm Hotel

HIGHLY COMMENDED

Tabor,
Dolgellau
LL40 2PS
Tel: (01341) 422361/422197
Fax: (01341) 422361

Secretly secluded overlooking the magnificent Mawddach Estuary stands Fronoleu. This family-run farm hotel combines traditional Welsh warmth with modern excellence. Log fired lounges, award winning restaurant, four poster beds, celtic harpist most evenings enhances Fronoleu's friendly and cosy atmosphere. Free fishing licenses, very lively at weekends and idyllically peaceful in the week.

P ♞ ♨ 🛏 🍽	SINGLE PER PERSON B&B		DOUBLE FOR 2 PERSONS B&B		🛏10 🛏6
	MIN £	MAX £	MIN £	MAX £	OPEN
	22.00	25.00	39.00	47.50	1-12

GH | Dwy Olwyn

HIGHLY COMMENDED

Coed-y-Fronallt,
Dolgellau
LL40 2YG
Tel: (01341) 422822

Situated in an acre of landscaped gardens, boasting magnificent views in a peaceful position yet only 10 minutes walk to the town. Within the Snowdonia National Park close to all amenities and numerous walks. Good home-cooking. Cleanliness and personal attention assured. Ample parking, TV and tea/coffee facilities in all bedrooms. Large guest lounge.

P 🛏 ♨✕ 🍽	SINGLE PER PERSON B&B		DOUBLE FOR 2 PERSONS B&B		🛏3 🛏–
	MIN £	MAX £	MIN £	MAX £	OPEN
	–	–	27.00	30.00	2-12

GH | Y Goedlan

COMMENDED

Brithdir,
Dolgellau
LL40 2RN
Tel: (01341) 423131
Fax: (01341) 423131

This old vicarage offers peaceful accommodation in pleasant rural surroundings. Ideally placed on B4416 road for walks, sea, mountains and touring. Spacious double, twin and family rooms, all with hot and cold, colour TV, central heating, tea/coffee facilities. Bathroom with shower, two conveniences. Lounge comfort with homely atmosphere. Hearty breakfast. Reduction for children. Dolgellau two miles.

P 🛏 ♨	SINGLE PER PERSON B&B		DOUBLE FOR 2 PERSONS B&B		🛏3 🛏–
	MIN £	MAX £	MIN £	MAX £	OPEN
	17.50	–	31.00	–	2-11

GH Rhaiadr Wnion

Rhyd-y-main,
Dolgellau
LL40 2AH
Tel: (01341) 450249

COMMENDED

Open 1-12

B&B pp Max £15.00, Double, B&B Max £30.00

GH Tanyfron

Arran Road,
Dolgellau
LL40 2AA
Tel: (01341) 422638
Fax: (01341) 422638

HIGHLY COMMENDED

A warm welcome awaits you in our comfortable, quiet, modernised 100 year old former farmhouse. Lovely views, half a mile from Dolgellau. Tastefully furnished with matching decor. All rooms have tea/coffee making, hairdryers, heating, clock radio and colour TV with sky channels. Laundry and public telephone. Parking in our own grounds. Non-smoking.

		SINGLE PER PERSON B&B		DOUBLE FOR 2 PERSONS B&B		
		MIN £	MAX £	MIN £	MAX £	OPEN
		–	–	36.00	38.00	2-11

FGH Arosfyr Farm

Penycefn Road,
Dolgellau
LL40 2YP
Tel: (01341) 422355

APPROVED

Open 1-12

B&B pp £16.00 - £18.00. Double, B&B £28.00 - £30.00

GH Trem Idris

LLanelltyd,
Nr Dolgellau
LL40 2TB
Tel: (01341) 423776

HIGHLY COMMENDED

Situated in an elevated position over-looking the outstandingly beautiful Mawddach Estuary and with extensive panoramic views of Cader Idris mountains. One standard, two en-suite rooms, one ground floor. All rooms with colour TV, tea/coffee facilities. Renowned for scenic walks. Ideally situated for exploring Snowdonia. Seven miles from the coast. Homely relaxed atmosphere. Non-smokers please.

		SINGLE PER PERSON B&B		DOUBLE FOR 2 PERSONS B&B		
		MIN £	MAX £	MIN £	MAX £	OPEN
		17.00	20.00	35.00	38.00	1-12

FH Cyfannedd Uchaf

Arthog
LL39 1LX
Tel: (01341) 250526

HIGHLY COMMENDED

A comfortable non-smoking farmhouse situated at 750ft in the foothills of the Cader Idris mountain range. Guests are invited to share the beamed lounge with a log fire on chilly evenings. Panoramic coastal and mountain views. Farmhouse suppers available. Children over 14 welcome. No pets. One of those hidden places. Grid ref SH635127.

		SINGLE PER PERSON B&B		DOUBLE FOR 2 PERSONS B&B		
		MIN £	MAX £	MIN £	MAX £	OPEN
		–	–	35.00	37.00	5-9

FGH Pentre Mawr Farm

Dyffryn Ardudwy,
LL44 2ES
Tel: (01341) 247413

HIGHLY COMMENDED

Relax in the peace and quiet of this comfortble, modernised stone farmhouse. Conveniently situated for local amenities such as golf, pony trekking, fishing, birdwatching, castles and lakes. Within easy, level walking distance for Cambrian coastline and village pubs. Pets welcome. Be as busy or as lazy as you like!

		SINGLE PER PERSON B&B		DOUBLE FOR 2 PERSONS B&B		
		MIN £	MAX £	MIN £	MAX £	OPEN
		19.00	23.00	32.00	42.00	3-11

GH Einion House

Friog,
Fairbourne
LL38 2NX
Tel: (01341) 250644

COMMENDED

Lovely old house set in beautiful scenery between mountains and the sea. Reputation for good home cooking. Vegetarians catered for. All bedrooms colour TV, clock radio, hairdryer, tea/coffee maker. Marvellous walking, pony trekking, fishing, birdwatching. Good centre for narrow gauge railways and castles. Safe sandy beach a few minutes walk from house.

		SINGLE PER PERSON B&B		DOUBLE FOR 2 PERSONS B&B		
		MIN £	MAX £	MIN £	MAX £	OPEN
		20.50	–	35.00	38.00	1-12

GH Tŷ Clwb

The Square,
Ffestiniog
LL41 4LS
Tel: (01766) 762658

HIGHLY COMMENDED

Amidst mountains, wooded valleys and close to the coast, Tŷ Clwb offers quality accommodation in a peaceful village. A tastefully modernised 18th century guest house, all bedrooms are en-suite and delightfully individual with mountain views. Large comfortable lounge with TV, south facing balcony overlooking beautiful countryside. A warm welcome and high standard guaranteed.

		SINGLE PER PERSON B&B		DOUBLE FOR 2 PERSONS B&B		
		MIN £	MAX £	MIN £	MAX £	OPEN
		20.00	24.00	34.00	40.00	1-12

H Estuary Motel

Talsarnau
LL47 6TA
Tel: (01766) 771155

HIGHLY COMMENDED

The motel with all the facilities of a hotel, family-run, close by glorious beaches, beautiful mountain scenery, golf courses, fishing, riding etc. Comfortable TV lounge, licensed bar and restaurant with excellent home-cooking. Ample car parking. Large discounts on three night breaks available. Brochure on request.

		SINGLE PER PERSON B&B		DOUBLE FOR 2 PERSONS B&B		
		MIN £	MAX £	MIN £	MAX £	OPEN
		20.00	25.00	40.00	50.00	2-12

Harlech Llanberis Caernarfon Machynlleth Porthmadog

GH | Glanygors

LLandanwg,
Harlech
LL46 2SD
Tel: (01341) 241410

HIGHLY COMMENDED

Small friendly rural setting guest house near to beach. Beautiful views of mountains, central location for Snowdonia National Park. Birdwatching, sailing, hill walking, riding all in the area. Presenting good home-cooking in a homely and relaxed atmosphere. Central heating and electric blanket for winter months. Open all year. Warm Welsh welcome.

P 🐾		SINGLE PER PERSON B&B		DOUBLE FOR 2 PERSONS B&B		🛏 3
📺 ♨ 📶						🛏 1
		MIN £ 14.00	MAX £ 15.00	MIN £ 28.00	MAX £ 30.00	OPEN 1-12

GH | Godre'r Graig

Ffordd Newydd,
Harlech
LL46 2UD
Tel: (01766) 780905

HIGHLY COMMENDED

Warm friendly welcome with mouth watering food as a bonus, including vegetarian choice. Nestling under Harlech Castle close to all local amenities. Ardudwy Theatre, Royal St Davids Golf Club, swimming pool, sauna just a couple of minutes away. Ideal for walkers, cyclists, pony trekking, fishing, freshwater or sea. Two mountain bikes for hire.

P 🐾		SINGLE PER PERSON B&B		DOUBLE FOR 2 PERSONS B&B		🛏 3
📺 ♨ 📶						🛏 –
		MIN £ 15.00	MAX £ 18.00	MIN £ 29.00	MAX £ 29.00	OPEN 1-12

FH | Tyddyn Perthi

Penisarwaen,
Caernarfon
LL55 3BY
Tel: (01286) 872444

HIGHLY COMMENDED

Situated in the foothills of Snowdon, a small family farm famed for its prize winning Welsh Black cattle. Ideally placed for hill walking, climbing, watersports, paragliding etc. Tastefully furnished rooms with tea/coffee making facilities. Hearty Welsh breakfast a speciality. Ample parking.

P 🐾		SINGLE PER PERSON B&B		DOUBLE FOR 2 PERSONS B&B		🛏 2
C 📺						🛏 2
♨		MIN £ 18.00	MAX £ 18.00	MIN £ 36.00	MAX £ 36.00	OPEN 1-12

GH | Maenllwyd

Newtown Road,
Machynlleth
SY20 8EY
Tel: (01654) 702928
Fax: (01654) 702928
E-mail: maenllwyd@dircon.co.uk

AWARD

HIGHLY COMMENDED

Open 1-12

B&B pp £23.00 - £25.00. Double, B&B £36.00 - £40.00

P 🐾 📺 ♨ 📶 | 🛏 8 🛏 8

FH | Mathafarn

Llanwrin,
Machynlleth
SY20 8QJ
Tel: (01650) 511226

HIGHLY COMMENDED

Henry VII is reputed to have stayed here en-route to the Battle of Bosworth. Now this 16th century elegant country house is part of a working farm. Inglenook fire, central heating, television lounge, single, twin, private bathroom, double en-suite. Tea/coffee making facilities. Close to Machynlleth, Centre for Alternative Technology. Beautiful coastline of Aberdovey. Contact Susan Hughes.

P 📺		SINGLE PER PERSON B&B		DOUBLE FOR 2 PERSONS B&B		🛏 3
♨						🛏 2
		MIN £ 20.00	MAX £ 20.00	MIN £ 36.00	MAX £ 40.00	OPEN 1-12

GH | Skellerns

35 Madoc Street,
Porthmadog
LL49 9BU
Tel: (01766) 512843

COMMENDED

Friendly welcome for all. Excellent Welsh breakfast or vegetarian breakfasts served. Heating, tea/coffee facilities and TV in all bedrooms. Keys supplied, special rates for children. Shops, buses, trains, cinema nearby. Ideally situated for visiting Portmeirion Italianate Village, Snowdonia Mountains, Ffestiniog Steam Railway and Black Rock Sands. Open all year. Contact proprietor Mrs R Skellern.

🐾 📺		SINGLE PER PERSON B&B		DOUBLE FOR 2 PERSONS B&B		🛏 3
♨						🛏 0
		MIN £ 12.50	MAX £ 14.00	MIN £ 25.00	MAX £ 28.00	OPEN 1-12

Discovering Accessible Wales

This publication is packed full of helpful information for visitors with disabilities. Subjects covered include attractions, accommodation and activities.

For your free copy please see the 'Guides and Maps' section of this book

Llanberis

Tal-y-llyn Tywyn

GH	Wenydd

Minffordd,
Penrhyndeudraeth
LL48 6EF
Tel: (01766) 771542
Fax: (01766) 771542

HIGHLY COMMENDED

Friendly comfortable modern family house in quiet village location near Portmeirion. Ideal touring and walking centre near sea and mountains. Newly furnished rooms all have mountain views, hot and cold, colour TV, tea makers, clock radios, central heating. Gourmet breakfasts with choice of menu. Private parking. All guests receive our personal attention. Brochure available.

P	🛏		SINGLE PER PERSON B&B		DOUBLE FOR 2 PERSONS B&B		🛏 3
			MIN £	MAX £	MIN £	MAX £	OPEN
			15.00	18.00	30.00	36.00	1-12

FGH	Yoke House Farm

Pwllheli
LL53 5TY
Tel: (01758) 612621

HIGHLY COMMENDED

A beautifully wooded drive welcomes you to this Georgian farmhouse on a 290 acre working farm where guests are invited to watch the milking, calf feeding etc. Tastefully furnished, the accommodation consists of one double and one twin bedded room all with wash-hand basins, shaver points and welcome tray. Exciting nature trail open to guests.

P			SINGLE PER PERSON B&B		DOUBLE FOR 2 PERSONS B&B		🛏 2
			MIN £	MAX £	MIN £	MAX £	OPEN
			16.50	17.00	33.00	34.00	4-10

FH	Dolffanog Fach

Tal-y-llyn,
Tywyn
LL36 9AJ
Tel: (01654) 761235
Fax: (01654) 761235

HIGHLY COMMENDED

Situated near Talyllyn Lake at the foot of Cader Idris, in the Snowdonia National Park. Three en-suite bedrooms with colour TV, tea/coffee making facilities and hairdryers. Good home-cooking, ideal touring centre, walking, fishing, trekking, Centre for Alternative Technology, labyrinth at Corris Craft Centre or climbing Cader Idris. Games room with full size snooker table. Enquiries Mrs Meirwen Pughe.

P	🛏		SINGLE PER PERSON B&B		DOUBLE FOR 2 PERSONS B&B		🛏 3
🍴			MIN £	MAX £	MIN £	MAX £	OPEN
			20.00	22.00	36.00	40.00	1-11

GH	Rhosydd

26 Glan Cymerau,
Pwllheli
LL53 5PU
Tel: (01758) 612956

COMMENDED

Open 1-12

B&B pp £13.50 - £15.00. Double, B&B Max £30.00

P	C	🛏			🍴		🛏 2	🛏 1

GH	Llys Caradog Guest House

Trefriw
LL27 0RQ
Tel: (01492) 640919

COMMENDED

Open 1-11

B&B pp £13.00 - £16.00. Double, B&B £26.00 - £32.00

P					🛏 4	🛏 -

FH	Eisteddfa

Abergynolwyn,
Tywyn
LL36 9UP
Tel: (01654) 782228 or
(01654) 782385

COMMENDED

GOLD

A new luxury bungalow built next to the farmhouse overlooking the Talyllyn Gauge Railway. En-suite bedrooms, central heating, beverage trays, TV lounge, log fire when cold and wet, home-cooking. 5 miles Tywyn, one and half miles from Abergynolwyn. We are approximately 600 yards off the B4405 between Abergynolwyn and Dolgoch Falls.

P	🛏		SINGLE PER PERSON B&B		DOUBLE FOR 2 PERSONS B&B		🛏 3
							🛏 3
🍴			MIN £	MAX £	MIN £	MAX £	OPEN
			16.00	18.00	24.00	32.00	3-11

Pwllheli

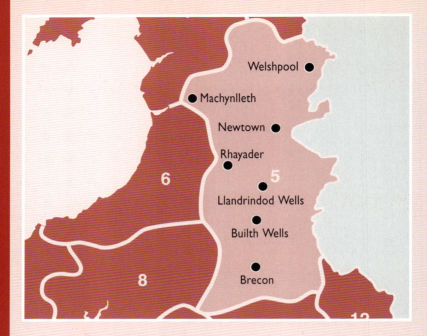

Welshpool

Machynlleth

Newtown

Rhayader

6

5

Llandrindod Wells

Builth Wells

8

Brecon

12

This large area encompasses the rural heartlands of Wales. From the unexplored Berwyn Mountains in the north to the grassy heights of the Brecon Beacons in the south, the predominant colour is green. And the predominant mood is restful, for this is Wales's most peaceful and unhurried area, a place of quiet country roads and small market towns, hill sheep farms and rolling borderlands. It's also a place of scenic lakes – the Elan Valley, Clywedog and Vyrnwy – set in undisturbed landscapes rich in wildlife, where you may spot the rare red kite circling in the skies. And Wales's great outdoors doesn't come any greater than in the Brecon Beacons National Park, whose wide, open spaces were made for walking and pony trekking.

Llyn Clywedog

It's a fact...

The Brecon Beacons National Park, covering 519 square miles, was designated in 1957. The Beacons' peak of Pen-y-fan, at 886m/2907ft, is the highest summit in South Wales. The Elan Valley reservoirs, created between 1892 and 1903, were the first of Wales's man-made lakelands. Llanwrtyd Wells appears in the Guinness Book of Records as the smallest town in Britain. Nineteenth-century diarist Francis Kilvert was curate of Clyro in the 1860s and '70s. Sections of the 8th-century earthwork known as Offa's Dyke – the first official border between England and Wales – still stand almost to their full height in the hills around Knighton.

Mc1　　Abergavenny

Flourishing market town with backdrop of mountains an south-eastern gateway to Brecon Beacons National Park. Pony trekking in nearby Black Mountains. Castle and museum; leisure centre. Monmouthshire and Brecon Canal runs just to the west. Excellent touring base for the lovely Vale of Usk and Brecon Beacons.

Ge6　　Brecon

Main touring centre for the 519 square miles of the Brecon Beacons National Park. Handsome old town with thriving market, ruined castle, cathedral (with its imaginative Heritage Centre), priory, theatre, three interesting museums (Brecknock, Jazz and South Wales Borderers) and Welsh Whisky Experience attraction. Wide range of inns and good shopping. Centre for walking and pony trekking. Golf, fishing and canal cruising also available. Very popular summer international Jazz Festival.

Ge4　　Builth Wells

Solidly built old country town which plays host every July to the Royal Welsh Agricultural Show, Wales's largest farming gathering. Lovely setting on River Wye amid beautiful hills. Lively sheep and cattle markets. Good shopping for local products, touring centre for Mid Wales and border country. River walk, Wyeside Arts Centre.

Hb7　　Crickhowell

Small, pleasant country town beautifully situated on the River Usk. Good for walking, fishing, pony trekking and riding. Remains of Norman castle. Nearby 14th-century Tretower Court and earlier castle also worth a visit.

Ha5　　Erwood

Small village on banks of the River Wye south-east of Builth Wells. Good base for fishing and walking - village is close to Brecon Beacons National Park, hills of central Wales and rolling border country.

Hb5　　Hay-on-Wye

Small market town on the Offa's Dyke Path, nestling below the Black Mountains on a picturesque stretch of the River Wye. A mecca for book lovers - there are antiquarian and second-hand bookshops, some huge, all over the town. Attractive crafts centre. Literature Festival in early summer attracts big names.

Hb2　　Knighton

Tref-y-Clawdd, the 'town on the dyke', stands in a deep wooded valley where the 8th-century Offa's Dyke defines the ancient border between Wales and England. Some of the best-preserved stretches of the earthen dyke can be found in the undisturbed hills near the town's Offa's Dyke Centre.

Ge3　　Llandrindod Wells

Victorian spa town with spacious streets and impressive architecture. Victorian-style visitor centre and excellent museum tracing the history of spa. Also has an intriguing museum dedicated to the bicycle. A popular inland resort with golf, fishing, bowling, boating and tennis available. Excellent touring centre for Mid Wales hills and lakes. Annual Victorian Festival in August.

Mb1　　Llangattock

Pretty village just across the River Usk from Crickhowell. Monmouthshire and Brecon Canal runs alongside. Spectacular walks (and caves) on the escarpment above. Handy base for all of the Brecon Beacons.

Ma1　　Llangynidr

This village in the Brecon Beacons National Park is approached from the south by a snaking mountain road with spectacular views. Pleasure boats ply along the nearby Monmouthshire and Brecon Canal. Good walking and fishing locally.

Ha5   Llyswen

Village in a lovely stretch of the upper Wye Valley between Builth Wells and Brecon. Good fishing locally and wonderful walking country - the Brecon Beacons and Black Mountains are on the doorstep. Hay-on-Wye, the 'town of books', nearby.

Dc5   Machynlleth

Historic market town near beautiful Dovey Estuary. Owain Glyndwr's Parliament House in the wide handsome main street is now a museum and brass rubbing centre. Superbly equipped Bro Ddyfi Leisure Centre offers wide range of activities. Celtica centre tells the story of Celtic myth and legend. Ancient and modern meet here; the inventive Centre for Alternative Technology is 3 miles away, just off the A487 to Dolgellau. Felin Crewi Flour Mill is off the A489 2 miles to the east.

Ec6   Montgomery

Hilltop market town of distinctive Georgian architecture beneath the ruins of a 13th-century castle. Offa's Dyke, which once marked the border, runs nearby. Not far from Welshpool and Powis Castle.

Hb3   New Radnor

Historic village in sleepy border country close to Offa's Dyke Path. Remnants of a medieval castle. Interesting old church at nearby Old Radnor. Radnor Forest to the north, Hay-on-Wye, the 'town of books', to the south.

Eb6   Newtown

Busy Severn Valley market town and one-time home of Welsh flannel industry. Textile history recalled in small museum; another museum based around Robert Owen, pioneer socialist, who lived here. Town also has interesting W H Smith Museum, solid old buildings, river promenade, street market and the lively Theatr Hafren.

Eb3   Penybontfawr

Secluded village amid forests and lakes, near the spectacular 73m/240ft Pistyll Rhaeadr waterfalls. Pony trekking and walking country, with hills and woods all around. Lake Vyrnwy Visitor Centre nearby.

Hc2   Presteigne

Typical black-and-white half-timbered border town with ancient inns; the Radnorshire Arms has secret passages. Judge's Lodging attraction recreates the past. Pony trekking available - the perfect way to explore this tranquil wooded countryside. Offa's Dyke Path nearby.

Gd2   Rhayader

Country market town full of character, with inviting inns and Welsh craft products in the shops. Excellent base for exploring mountains and lakes (Elan Valley and Claerwen), with opportunities for pony trekking, mountain biking and fishing. Welsh Royal Crystal Visitor Centre. Small museum. An interesting walk through the country on the nearby Gigrin Farm Trail.

Ma1   Talybont-on-Usk

Village in pastoral setting in Usk Valley on Monmouthshire and Brecon Canal. Attractive canalside inns. Within the Brecon Beacons National Park. Surrounding hills perfect for walking and pony trekking.

Ec5   Welshpool

Old market town of the borderlands, full of character, with half-timbered buildings and welcoming inns. Attractive canalside museum. Good shopping centre - especially at the Old Station, a major shopping venue; also golf and angling. Powis Castle is an impressive stately home with a Clive of India Museum and outstanding gardens. Ride the narrow-gauge Welshpool and Llanfair Light Railway, visit the Moors Wildlife Collection.

H Rock and Fountain Hotel

Clydach
Abergavenny
NP7 0LL
Tel: (01873) 830393 COMMENDED

Brecon Beacons National Park, 16th century family-run hotel, situated in the famous Clydach Gorge. The hotel has breathtaking views with riding, golf, fishing, and canal boating nearby. The beautiful featured restaurant offers home-cooked meals using fresh local produce. Lovely walks in a tranquil setting pass the front door. These you must try.

P	♀	SINGLE PER PERSON B&B		DOUBLE FOR 2 PERSONS B&B		🛏 9
🍴	🚿					🛏 9
🍽		MIN £ 20.00	MAX £ 25.00	MIN £ 38.00	MAX £ 40.00	OPEN 1-12

H Bishops Meadow Motel

Hay Road,
Brecon LD3 9SW
Tel: (01874) 622051/622392
Fax: (01874) 622428 🚶 COMMENDED

Open 1-12
B&B Double Min £46.00
| P 🐾 C ♀ 🍴 🍽 | | 🛏 20 🛏 20 |

H Tai'r Bull Inn

Libanus,
Brecon
LD3 8EL
Tel: (01874) 625849 HIGHLY COMMENDED

In the heart of the Brecon Beacons National Park, ideal for walking or touring, close to the Mountain Centre, Pen-y-fan and many other attractions. All our rooms are en-suite and we have car parking. Good food available all week in our oak beamed bar or dining room. Packed lunches on request.

P	♀	SINGLE PER PERSON B&B		DOUBLE FOR 2 PERSONS B&B		🛏 5
🍴	🚿					🛏 5
🍽		MIN £ 20.00	MAX £ 25.00	MIN £ 40.00	MAX £ 40.00	OPEN 1-12

GH The Beacons

16 Bridge Street,
Brecon
LD3 8AH
Tel: (01874) 623339
Fax: (01874) 623339  COMMENDED

Recently restored Georgian house with cellar bar, lounge and private parking. Comfortable rooms, mostly en-suite with many 'extras'. Four poster and king-size luxury rooms also available. Restaurant with excellent cuisine from award-winning chef. Wonderfully situated for town centre, river walks, Brecon Beacons and Black Mountains. Ring Peter or Barbara Jackson. AAQQQ. RAC Acclaimed.

P	♀	SINGLE PER PERSON B&B		DOUBLE FOR 2 PERSONS B&B		🛏 12
♀	🍴					🛏 9
🚿	🍽	MIN £ 18.00	MAX £ 25.00	MIN £ 36.00	MAX £ 42.00	OPEN 1-12

GH Cambridge House

St David Street,
Brecon
LD3 8BB
Tel: (01874) 624699 HIGHLY COMMENDED
GOLD

Open 1-12
B&B pp Max £16.00. Double, B&B £30.00 - £34.00
| P 🐾 🍴 🚿 🍽 | | 🛏 4 🛏 1 |

GH The Coach Guest House

Orchard Street,
Brecon
LD3 8AN
Tel: (01874) 623803 HIGHLY COMMENDED

'Hotel standards at guest house prices' Six bedrooms all en-suite, three with bath, three with shower. Four double rooms, two twin. All have colour TV, hairdryer, clock radio, telephone and beverage tray. Whole house completely non-smoking. Ideal base for touring Brecon Beacons National Park. Close to town centre. RAC Highly Acclaimed. AAQQQ.

P	♀	SINGLE PER PERSON B&B		DOUBLE FOR 2 PERSONS B&B		🛏 6
🍴	🚿					🛏 6
🍽		MIN £ –	MAX £ –	MIN £ 40.00	MAX £ 42.00	OPEN 1-12

GH Glascwm

Talyllyn,
Brecon
LD3 7SY
Tel: (01874) 658649 HIGHLY COMMENDED

Fine Edwardian country guest house nestling in rural community close to Llangorse Lake amid the majestic Brecon Beacons and awe inspiring Black Mountains. A family run non-smoking establishment with excellent facilities set in 4 acres of countryside. Children most welcome and well catered for. The Glascwm breakfast our speciality.

P	♀	SINGLE PER PERSON B&B		DOUBLE FOR 2 PERSONS B&B		🛏 3
🍴	🚿					🛏 3
🍽		MIN £ 20.00	MAX £ 25.00	MIN £ 38.00	MAX £ 42.00	OPEN 1-11

FH Maeswalter

Heol Senni,
Nr Brecon
LD3 8SU
Tel: (01874) 636629 COMMENDED

Set in a picturesque and quiet sheep farming valley of Heol Senni. This 17th century farmhouse offers a warm welcome and friendly atmosphere where guests return again and again. There are just three tastefully decorated bedrooms, including one family room. The beamed lounge is for guests which also serves as a dining room.

P	🐾	SINGLE PER PERSON B&B		DOUBLE FOR 2 PERSONS B&B		🛏 3
🍴	🍽					🛏 1
		MIN £ 20.00	MAX £ 25.00	MIN £ 35.00	MAX £ 38.00	OPEN 1-12

GH The Old Rectory

Llanddew,
Brecon
LD3 9SS
Tel: (01874) 622058 HIGHLY COMMENDED

Peacefully situated in 2 acres of its own grounds the Old Rectory is half a mile north of Brecon. Magnificent views of the Brecon Beacons. Every comfort provided for, central heating, colour TV, tea/coffee all rooms. A warm welcome is assured and personal service. Pony trekking, golf, fishing all nearby. Ample parking. Self-catering cottage in grounds.

P	🍴	SINGLE PER PERSON B&B		DOUBLE FOR 2 PERSONS B&B		🛏 3
🚿						🛏 2
		MIN £ 20.00	MAX £ –	MIN £ –	MAX £ 40.00	OPEN 1-12

Cyclists and Walkers Welcome

Look out for the 'boot' and 'bike' symbols. They are displayed by places which have undertaken to provide features which cyclists and/or walkers always find welcome. These include drying facilities for wet clothes and boots, secure lockable area for bikes, availability of packed lunches and so on. You'll even be greeted with a welcoming cup of tea or coffee on arrival.

Brecon Builth Wells Crickhowell

GH | **Tir Bach Guest House**

13 Alexandra Road,
Brecon
LD3 7PD
Tel: (01874) 624551

COMMENDED

On quiet road overlooking town, with panoramic Brecon Beacons view. Only 2 minutes leisurely walk fron Brecon town centre. Family-run guest house. Spacious lounge, all rooms colour TV and tea/coffee making facilities, central heating. Car parking. First class traditional British breakfast. Special rates for children. Well travelled friendly hosts. Relaxing atmosphere. (no sign).

P 🐕 ⊞		SINGLE PER PERSON B&B		DOUBLE FOR 2 PERSONS B&B		🛏 3 🛏 –
		MIN £ 16.00	MAX £ 16.00	MIN £ 30.00	MAX £ 34.00	OPEN 2-11

FGH | **The Tower**

Scethrog,
Brecon
LD3 7YE
Tel: (01874) 676672
Fax: (0181) 960 8246

COMMENDED

Romantic, medieval house surrounded by meadows, mountains and river. Two spacious oak beamed bed-sitting rooms each with en-suite washroom and toilet, colour TV, fridge, tea/coffee facilities. Large garden for picnics overlooking Kingfisher pond. Relaxed atmosphere, late breakfast if required. Steep stone steps. Private trout fishing. Guest telephone.

P 🐕 ⊞ 🍴		SINGLE PER PERSON B&B		DOUBLE FOR 2 PERSONS B&B		🛏 2 🛏 2
		MIN £ 20.00	MAX £ 24.00	MIN £ 32.00	MAX £ 38.00	OPEN 3-10

FH | **Bryn y Fedwen Farm**

Trallong Common
Sennybridge,
Brecon LD3 8HW
Tel: (01874) 636505
Fax: (01874) 636505

HIGHLY COMMENDED

AWARD

GOLD

Bryn y Fedwen is situated high above the river Usk Valley amidst lovely countryside, with panoramic views of the Brecon Beacons. Enjoy a warm friendly atmosphere, spacious en-suite bedrooms, including apartment for disabled visitors. Cosy lounge with log fire. Good home-cooking. Great for walking and birdwatching. Many attractions and activities close by.

P ⊞ 🍴		SINGLE PER PERSON B&B		DOUBLE FOR 2 PERSONS B&B		🛏 3 🛏 3
		MIN £ 22.00	MAX £ 22.00	MIN £ 40.00	MAX £ 40.00	OPEN 1-12

FH | **Cwmcamlais Uchaf Farm**

Cwmcamlais,
Sennybridge, Brecon
LD3 8TD
Tel: (01874) 636376
Fax: (01874) 636376

HIGHLY COMMENDED

Cwmcamlais Uchaf is a working farm situated in the Brecon Beacons National Park, one mile off the A40 between Brecon and Sennybridge. Our 16th century farmhouse has exposed beams and stonework inglenook fireplace and tastefully decorated bedrooms, 2 en-suite with tea/coffee making facilities. The river Camlais with its waterfalls flows through our farmland. A warm Welsh welcome awaits you.

P 🐕 ⊞ 🐴 🍴		SINGLE PER PERSON B&B		DOUBLE FOR 2 PERSONS B&B		🛏 3 🛏 2
		MIN £ 19.00	MAX £ 22.00	MIN £ 36.00	MAX £ 40.00	OPEN 1-12

FH | **Llanbrynean Farm**

LLanfrynach,
Brecon
LD3 7BY
Tel: (01874) 665333

COMMENDED

Come and relax in the heart of the Brecon Beacons in our charismatic, old farmhouse with spacious accommodation and homely relaxed atmosphere. Situated on the edge of a quiet, picturesque village offering excellent pub food. We have wonderful pastoral views and a large garden. Tea/coffee facilites. Sitting room with log fire and TV. Working family farm.

P 🐕 🐴		SINGLE PER PERSON B&B		DOUBLE FOR 2 PERSONS B&B		🛏 3 🛏 2
		MIN £ 18.00	MAX £ 20.00	MIN £ 32.00	MAX £ 37.00	OPEN 3-11

FGH | **New Hall**

LLanddewircwm,
Builth Wells
LD2 3RX
Tel: (01982) 552483

HIGHLY COMMENDED

AWARD

Situated one and a half miles from Builth Wells and Royal Welsh Showground on B4520 road. Magnificent unspoilt scenery overlooking the Wye valley. Picturesque walking area, paragliding, mountain biking. Centrally situated for places and activities in central Wales. Easy access parking. Ground floor bedrooms, Comfortable accommodation in 17th century farmhouse renovated to a high standard. Brochure.

P ⊞ 🐴 🍴		SINGLE PER PERSON B&B		DOUBLE FOR 2 PERSONS B&B		🛏 3 🛏 3
		MIN £ 20.00	MAX £ 22.00	MIN £ 40.00	MAX £ 44.00	OPEN 1-12

FH | **Dollynwydd Farm**

Builth Wells
LD2 3RZ
Tel: (01982) 553660

COMMENDED

GOLD

17th century farmhouse lying beneath the Eppynt Hills. Wonderful area for walking, touring and birdwatching. Within easy distance of Brecon Beacons, Elan Valley, Hay-on-Wye bookshops. Very comfortable, log fire, oak beams. Home-cooking with fresh produce. Ample car parking, attractive garden. One mile from Builth Wells B4520 first left, signed Tregare Erwood, house on left, 200 yards down farm lane.

P 🐴 🐕 🍴		SINGLE PER PERSON B&B		DOUBLE FOR 2 PERSONS B&B		🛏 3 🛏 3
		MIN £ 16.00	MAX £ 16.00	MIN £ 32.00	MAX £ 40.00	OPEN 2-11

FH | **Tŷ Isaf Farm**

Erwood,
Builth Wells
LD2 3SZ
Tel: (01982) 560607

COMMENDED

Open 1-12

B&B pp £14.00 - £15.00. Double, B&B £28.00 - £30.00

P 🐕 C ⊞ 🐴 🍴   🛏 3 🛏 –

H | **Stables Hotel**

Neuadd,
Llangattock,
Crickhowell NP8 1LE
Tel: (01873) 810244

HIGHLY COMMENDED

High class internationally known country hotel situated in 30 acres of gardens and grounds. Restaurant with Wales' largest fireplace. Superb cooking with fresh local produce our speciality, all main meals served with six fresh vegetables. New Trelawneg suites, four poster beds and chateau style rooms, conservatory suites. Short breaks to include dinner. RAC Acclaimed.

P 🐕 🍷 ⊞ 🐴 🍴		SINGLE PER PERSON B&B		DOUBLE FOR 2 PERSONS B&B		🛏 14 🛏 14
		MIN £ –	MAX £ 25.00	MIN £ –	MAX £ –	OPEN 1-12

FH | **Cwrt Isaf Farm**

Llangattock,
Nr Crickhowell
NP8 1PH
Tel: (01873) 812128
Tel: (01873) 812129

AWAITING GRADING

Open 1-12

B&B pp Min £22.50. Double, B&B Min £45.00

P ⊞ 🐴 🍴   🛏 3 🛏 3

GH | Old Vicarage

Erwood,
Builth Wells
LD2 3SZ
Tel: (01982) 560680

COMMENDED

GOLD

Former vicarage sitting in peaceful grounds, stunning views from spacious attractive rooms with double aspects and period furnishings. Bedrooms have drinks tray, C.H, handbasins and period beds and bedcovers a special feature. Guests own bathroom and separate toilet. Private TV lounge, indoor games, separate dining room own produce from our garden. Children and pets welcome. River walks. Elan Valley, Brecon Beacons, Hay-on-Wye and Black Mountains nearby.

P 🐕		SINGLE PER PERSON B&B	DOUBLE FOR 2 PERSONS B&B	🛏 3
C 🛏				🛏 –
🛁 🍽		MIN £	MAX £	MIN £	MAX £	OPEN
		14.00	15.00	28.00	30.00	1-12

GH | The Old Post Office

Llanigon,
Hay-on-Wye
HR3 5QA
Tel: (01497) 820008

COMMENDED

17th century Grade 2 listed house in a quiet rural location only two miles from the famous book town Hay-on-Wye. Set in the lovely Brecon Becons National Park at the foot of the Black Mountains. Offas Dyke path close by. Superb vegetarian breakfast, guests own sitting room and lovely bedrooms. Recommended by the "Which?" B&B guide.

P 🐕	SINGLE PER PERSON B&B	DOUBLE FOR 2 PERSONS B&B	🛏 3
🛏 🍽			🛏 2
	MIN £	MAX £	MIN £	MAX £	OPEN
	17.00	25.00	30.00	40.00	2-12

FGH | Cefnsuran Farmhouse

Llangunllo,
Knighton
LD7 1SL
Tel: (01547) 550219
Fax: (01547) 550219

HIGHLY COMMENDED

16th century 300 acre working farm in isolated valley. Peaceful large open plan garden, extremely picturesque countryside, accommodation maintained to a high modern standard, retaining its farmhouse feel. Traditional and gourmet cooking, vegetarian and special diets catered for. Local fresh produce used. Leisure facilities within 6 miles, fishing on farm, walks. Warm welcome awaits.

P 🍷		SINGLE PER PERSON B&B	DOUBLE FOR 2 PERSONS B&B	🛏 4
🛏 🍽				🛏 4
🍽		MIN £	MAX £	MIN £	MAX £	OPEN
		22.00	25.00	40.00	45.00	1-12

GH | Corven Hall

Howey,
Llandrindod Wells
LD1 5RE
Tel: (01597) 823368

HIGHLY COMMENDED

Victorian country house in large grounds surrounded by beautiful countryside one and half miles south of Llandrindod Wells, off A483 at Hundred House turn. The house is licensed, centrally heated, spacious TV lounge bar, most bedrooms en-suite, TV, tea/coffee facilities, ground floor accommodation. Traditional home-cooking, freshly prepared. Dinner by arrangement. Brochure available.

P 🐕	SINGLE PER PERSON B&B	DOUBLE FOR 2 PERSONS B&B	🛏 10
🍷 🛏			🛏 8
🛏 🍽	MIN £	MAX £	MIN £	MAX £	OPEN
	23.00	25.00	35.00	39.00	2-10

H | The Llanerch 16th Century Inn

Llanerch Lane,
Llandrindod Wells
LD1 6BG
Tel: (01597) 822086
Fax: (01597) 824618

HIGHLY COMMENDED

Come and relax in the traditional atmosphere and hospitality. Bedrooms have modern day comforts, tea/coffee making facilities, en-suite, telephone, radio etc. Excellent selection of meals, traditional ales, good wine list, beer garden, terrace, childrens' play area. Close to town centre and set in its own grounds. Families welcome. Plenty of parking.

P 🐕		SINGLE PER PERSON B&B	DOUBLE FOR 2 PERSONS B&B	🛏 12
C 🍷				🛏 12
🛏 🍽		MIN £	MAX £	MIN £	MAX £	OPEN
		–	–	45.00	49.00	1-12

GH | The Park Motel

Crossgates,
Llandrindod Wells
LD1 6RF
Tel: (01597) 851201
Fax: (01597) 851201

COMMENDED

Open 2-12

B&B pp £17.00 - £25.00. Double, B&B £34.00 - £46.00

P 🐕 🍷 🛏 🍽   🛏 7 🛏 7

GH | Greenglades Guest House

Llanyre,
Llandrindod Wells
LD1 6EA
Tel: (01597) 822950

HIGHLY COMMENDED

Open 1-12

B&B pp £20.00 - £22.00. Double, B&B £36.00 - £40.00

P 🛏 🍽   🛏 2 🛏 2

FH | Holly Farm

Howey,
Llandrindod Wells
LD1 5PP
Tel: (01597) 822402

AWARD

HIGHLY COMMENDED

GOLD

Working farm with charming old farmhouse dates back to Tudor times. Country lovers retreat, glorious unspoilt countryside, near scenic lakes and mountains, ideal for walking, birdwatching or relaxing. En-suite rooms, beverage trays, two lounges, TV, log fire. Home-cooking a speciality using farm produce. Tourism award. Safe parking. Evening meals by arrangement. Brochure, Mrs Ruth Jones.

P 🛏		SINGLE PER PERSON B&B	DOUBLE FOR 2 PERSONS B&B	🛏 5
🛁 🍽				🛏 3
		MIN £	MAX £	MIN £	MAX £	OPEN
		18.00	20.00	34.00	40.00	4-11

River Wye

43

Llandrindod Wells Llangattock Llangynidr Machynlleth Llyswen Montgomery New Radnor

---

FGH Neuadd Farm Country Guest House

HIGHLY COMMENDED

Penybont,
Llandrindod Wells
LD1 5SW
Tel: (01597) 822571
Fax: (01597) 822571

Enjoy a relaxing break in our comfortably furnished 16th century farmhouse overlooking the lovely Ithon Valley. Separate guest sitting and dining room, both with inglenook fireplaces. Good traditional home-cooking. Ideal for exploring Mid Wales and the Elan Valley or walk direct from our door. Brochure available.

P		SINGLE PER PERSON B&B		DOUBLE FOR 2 PERSONS B&B		🛏 3 🛏 3
		MIN £	MAX £	MIN £	MAX £	OPEN
		19.50	21.00	39.00	42.00	1-12

GH The Old Six Bells

COMMENDED

Llangattock,
Crickhowell
NP8 1PH
Tel: (01873) 811965
Fax: (01873) 811965

Old house with parts dating back to the 17th century and with many original features. Situated in the attractive village of Llangattock very close to Crickhowell. All rooms en-suite. Ideal base for touring Brecon Beacons National Park and beautiful Usk and Wye Valley.

P		SINGLE PER PERSON B&B		DOUBLE FOR 2 PERSONS B&B		🛏 2 🛏 2
		MIN £	MAX £	MIN £	MAX £	OPEN
		25.00	25.00	40.00	40.00	1-12

H The Red Lion Hotel

AWAITING GRADING

Duffryn Road,
Llangynidr, Crickhowell
NP8 1NT
Tel: (01874) 730223
Fax: (01874) 730992

15th century inn, nestling in the hills of Brecon Beacons National Park in the picturesque village of Llangynidr. The traditional charm of the inn is echoed throughout the interior with genuine beams, stone walls and open fire places. Within walking distance of the Brecon and Monmouthshire Canal and River Usk. Pony trekking, canoeing, fishing, windsurfing and hang gliding, facilities nearby.

P	C	SINGLE PER PERSON B&B		DOUBLE FOR 2 PERSONS B&B		🛏 - 🛏 -
		MIN £	MAX £	MIN £	MAX £	OPEN
		20.00	20.00	40.00	40.00	1-12

GH Oakfield

HIGHLY COMMENDED

Llyswen,
Brecon
LD3 0UR
Tel: (01874) 754301

Situated in the heart of the Wye Valley and Brecon Beacons National Park close to the market towns of Brecon, Builth Wells and Hay-on-Wye. Quiet family guest house with spacious rooms, one en-suite, lovely views and ample parking. Set back off the main A470. Central point for walking, pony trekking and canoeing.

P		SINGLE PER PERSON B&B		DOUBLE FOR 2 PERSONS B&B		🛏 2 🛏 1
		MIN £	MAX £	MIN £	MAX £	OPEN
		15.00	18.00	30.00	35.00	4-10

GH Felin Crewi

HIGHLY COMMENDED

Penegoes,
Machynlleth
SY20 8NH
Tel: (01654) 703113

Open 1-12

B&B pp £20.00 - £22.00. Double, B&B £36.00 - £44.00

GH Pendre Guest House

COMMENDED

Maengwyn Street,
Machynlleth
SY20 8EF
Tel: (01654) 702008

Open 1-12

B&B Double £33.00 - £37.00

FH The Drewin Farm

HIGHLY COMMENDED

GOLD

Churchstoke,
Montgomery
SY15 6TW
Tel: (01588) 620325

Open 4-10

B&B pp Max £20.00. Double, B&B £34.00 - £36.00

FH Little Brompton Farm

HIGHLY COMMENDED

GOLD

Montgomery
SY15 6HY
Tel: (01686) 668371

Country lovers retreat, glorious unspoilt countryside, quiet roads, stay at our charming 17th century farmhouse on working farm. Traditionally furnished oak beamed rooms, double, twin or family en-suites available. Colour TV, beverage trays, radio, hairdryers. Quality prevails. Good home-cooking. We are situated on the B4385 2 miles east of Montgomery, Offas Dyke runs through farm, Croeso.

P		SINGLE PER PERSON B&B		DOUBLE FOR 2 PERSONS B&B		🛏 3 🛏 3
C		MIN £	MAX £	MIN £	MAX £	OPEN
		–	–	38.00	40.00	1-12

H Red Lion

APPROVED

Llanfihangel Nant Melan,
New Radnor
LD8 2TN
Tel: (01544) 350220

Open 1-11

B&B pp Max £18.00. Double, B&B Max £35.00

Llandrindod Wells

GH | Brook Mill

Mochdre Lane,
Newtown
SY16 4JS
Tel: (01686) 624679

AWAITING GRADING

Set on the banks of a trout stream in the wooded Mochdre Valley, this 200 year old flannel mill has been converted to a high standard. A bridle path starting in the grounds leads the walker south along the Mochdre Brook, with course and game fishing in tranquil surroundings nearby.

P ♥ ▥ ☞		SINGLE PER PERSON B&B		DOUBLE FOR 2 PERSONS B&B		🛏 3 🛁 –
		MIN £	MAX £	MIN £	MAX £	OPEN
		20.00	20.00	40.00	40.00	1-12

FGH | Lletty Deryn

Mochdre,
Newtown
SY16 4JY
Tel: (01686) 626131

HIGHLY COMMENDED
GOLD

Restored 18th century farmhouse part of a working farm, rearing sheep and beef. Features include inglenook fireplace, exposed beams and traditional parlour. All rooms en-suite with superb views. All bread home-baked, vegetarians catered for. Not licensed but welcome to bring own bottle – we provide corkscrew. Off A489/470 west of Newtown.

P ▥ ❚ 🍴		SINGLE PER PERSON B&B		DOUBLE FOR 2 PERSONS B&B		🛏 3 🛁 3
		MIN £	MAX £	MIN £	MAX £	OPEN
		–	25.00	36.00	40.00	1-12

FH | Penyceunant

Penybontfawr
SY10 0PF
Tel: (01691) 860459

HIGHLY COMMENDED

Old farmhouse with spectacular views across the Tanat Valley. Substantial rooms with washbasin, colour TV and easy chair. Guests garden lounge. An ideal secluded retreat, yet well placed for touring. We specialise in walking holidays offering half board packages for week or weekend breaks. Information service, route card loan. Enquiries, brochure Anna Francis.

P ♥ ▥ ❚ 🍴		SINGLE PER PERSON B&B		DOUBLE FOR 2 PERSONS B&B		🛏 2 🛁 –
		MIN £	MAX £	MIN £	MAX £	OPEN
		–	18.00	–	30.00	1-11

GH | Greenfields

Kerry,
Newtown
SY16 4LH
Tel: (01686) 670596
Fax: (01686) 670354

COMMENDED

A warm welcome awaits you at our home. Spacious bedrooms have picturesque views of the rolling hills of Kerry, all bedrooms are en-suite and have colour TV. The lounge has open log fire when weather demands and colour TV. There is ample private parking. Taste of Wales member, brochure available contact, Vi Madeley.

P ♥ ❚ ▥ ❚ 🍴		SINGLE PER PERSON B&B		DOUBLE FOR 2 PERSONS B&B		🛏 3 🛁 3
		MIN £	MAX £	MIN £	MAX £	OPEN
		17.50	20.00	35.00	40.00	1-12

FH | Dyffryn Farmhouse

Aberhafesp,
Newtown
SY16 3JD
Tel: (01686) 688817
Fax: (01686) 688834

DE LUXE
AWARD

Luxury en-suite accommodation in 17th century farmhouse with exposed beams and delightful decor. Walks on 200 acre farm, lakes nearby. Delicious farmhouse fare with vegetarian specialities. Totally non-smoking. Warm welcome guaranteed – come and enjoy farmhouse hospitality amongst beautiful scenery – Kites and Badgers seen in area. Facilties for cyclists and walkers.

P ▥ ❚ 🍴		SINGLE PER PERSON B&B		DOUBLE FOR 2 PERSONS B&B		🛏 3 🛁 3
		MIN £	MAX £	MIN £	MAX £	OPEN
		24.00	26.00	44.00	48.00	1-12

FH | Willey Lodge Farm

Presteigne
LD8 2WB
Tel: (01544) 267341

COMMENDED

Open 2-11

B&B pp £15.00 - £18.00. Double, B&B £30.00 - £36.00

P ♥ ▥ 🍴	🛏 2 🛁 2

GH | Hillside Lodge Guest House

Llanbadarn Fynydd,
Nr Newtown
LD1 6TU
Tel: (01597) 840364
Fax: (01597) 840364

HIGHLY COMMENDED

Spacious and peaceful, this family-run guest house offers excellent accommodation in an outstanding position standing alone on the hillside. Looks out across the Ithon Valley. Ideal for long holidays or short peaceful breaks. Families welcome, pets by arrangement. All rooms en-suite, tea/coffee, hairdryers, ironing facilities. Elan Valley for fishing, birdwatching. Totally non-smoking.

P ♥ ▥ ❚ 🍴		SINGLE PER PERSON B&B		DOUBLE FOR 2 PERSONS B&B		🛏 3 🛁 3
		MIN £	MAX £	MIN £	MAX £	OPEN
		23.00	23.00	40.00	40.00	1-12

FH | Lower-Gwestydd

Newtown
SY16 3AY
Tel: (01686) 626718

HIGHLY COMMENDED
AWARD

Open 1-12

B&B pp £21.00 - £25.00. Double, B&B £38.00 - £40.00

P ▥ 🍴	🛏 2 🛁 2

H | Brynafon Country House Hotel

South Street,
Rhayader
LD6 5BL
Tel: (01597) 810735
Tel: (01597) 810111

COMMENDED

Uniquely situated amid the glorious hills and mountains yet only half a mile from Rhayader and modern leisure centre. Come and discover the famed comfort and charm of this former 'workhouse' and experience our renowned friendliness, warm welcome and excellent food. See the rare 'Red Kite' being fed on the neighbouring working farm.

P ♥ C ❚ ▥ 🍴		SINGLE PER PERSON B&B		DOUBLE FOR 2 PERSONS B&B		🛏 22 🛁 8
		MIN £	MAX £	MIN £	MAX £	OPEN
		10.00	25.00	32.00	50.00	1-12

Rhayader Talybont-on-Usk Welshpool

GH | **Brynteg Guest House**

East Street,
Rhayader
LD6 5EA
Tel: (01597) 810052

COMMENDED

Open 1-12

B&B pp Max £15.00. Double, B&B Max £30.00

P 🐕 ⏹ 🛏4 🛏4 *i*

PLEASE NOTE

All accommodation in this publication has
applied for grading. However, at the time of
going to press not all establishments had been
visited - some of these properties are indicated
by the wording
'AWAITING GRADING'

FH | **Gigrin Farm**

South Street,
Rhayader
LD6 5BL
Tel: (01597) 810243
Fax: (01597) 810357

COMMENDED

*A warm welcome awaits you at 'Gigrin' 198 acre
stock farm with two mile nature trail overlooking the
Wye Valley. The 17th century longhouse retains
original oak beams and cosy atmosphere. Half a mile
south of Rhayader just off A470. OS map 147 GR
980677. 'Red Kite' feeding takes place from mid
October to mid April at 2pm daily.*

i

P	⏹	SINGLE PER PERSON B&B		DOUBLE FOR 2 PERSONS B&B		🛏 3
✂						🛏 1
		MIN £	MAX £	MIN £	MAX £	OPEN
		17.50	20.00	35.00	35.00	1-12

H | **Belvedere**

Station Road,
Talybont-on-Usk,
Powys
LD3 7JE
Tel: (01874) 676264

HIGHLY COMMENDED

*Modern friendly very clean family business designed
and built by ourselves. Set between the Brecon
Beacons and the Black Mountains. All rooms have TV,
tea/coffee facilities, some en-suite. Short walk to
canal, River Usk, restaurants. Activities, pony trekking,
cycling, hill walking and fishing. Breathtaking
panoramic views, also local leisure centre and
Dan-Yr-Ogof showcaves.*

i

P	⏹	SINGLE PER PERSON B&B		DOUBLE FOR 2 PERSONS B&B		🛏 3
✂						🛏 1
		MIN £	MAX £	MIN £	MAX £	OPEN
		–	–	32.00	36.00	1-12

GH | **The Horseshoe Guest House**

Church Street,
Rhayader
LD6 5AT
Tel: (01597) 810982

HIGHLY COMMENDED

*A warm welcome awaits you at The Horseshoe a
large 200 year old Welsh stone house with beams
and log fire. We offer stylish, clean comfortable
accommodation, en-suite available. Situated in the
old part of Rhayader, three minutes to River Wye,
three miles to the magical Elan Valley. Ideal base for
exploring beautiful Mid Wales.*

i

P	🐕	SINGLE PER PERSON B&B		DOUBLE FOR 2 PERSONS B&B		🛏 5
⏹	✂					🛏 2
🍴		MIN £	MAX £	MIN £	MAX £	OPEN
		15.00	15.00	30.00	33.00	2-11

GH | **Abercynafon Lodge**

Abercynafon,
Nr Talybont-on-Usk,
Brecon
LD3 7YT
Tel: (01874) 676342

HIGHLY COMMENDED
GOLD

*Delightful rural B&B, idyllically situated at the head of
Talybont Reservoir. A painters paradise, a walkers
dream and a tourists haven. Come and be pampered,
relax and unwind. Excellent accommodation and
friendly hosts. We look forward to meeting you.*

i

P	🐕	SINGLE PER PERSON B&B		DOUBLE FOR 2 PERSONS B&B		🛏 2
⏹	✂					🛏 2
		MIN £	MAX £	MIN £	MAX £	OPEN
		16.00	16.00	32.00	36.00	1-12

FGH | **Tynllwyn Farm**

Welshpool
SY21 9BW
Tel: (01938) 553175/553054

HIGHLY COMMENDED

*Tynllwyn is a family farm and farmhouse with a
friendly welcome. Good farmhouse food and bar
license. All bedrooms have central heating, colour TV,
tea/coffee facilities, hot and cold wash units. One mile
from lovely market town of Welshpool on the A490
north. Very quiet and pleasantly situated on a hillside
with beautiful views. Two day short break available
October to March. Pets by arrangement.*

i

P	🐕	SINGLE PER PERSON B&B		DOUBLE FOR 2 PERSONS B&B		🛏 4
♟	⏹					🛏 1
✂	🍴	MIN £	MAX £	MIN £	MAX £	OPEN
		16.00	20.00	31.00	35.00	1-12

GH | **Liverpool House**

East Street
Rhayader LD6 5EA
Tel: (01597) 810706
Fax: (01597) 810356
E-mail: liverpoolhouse@compuserve.com

COMMENDED

*A warm welcome awaits you at Liverpool House,
mostly en-suite rooms, four poster beds available. All
bedrooms with colour TV, beverage tray, radio/alarm
clock, hairdryer and iron. Private secure parking. Cot
and highchair available. Excellent accommodation
either in main house or newly refurbished annexe.
Fire certificate. Families welcome. Reduced rates for
children.*

i

P	🐕	SINGLE PER PERSON B&B		DOUBLE FOR 2 PERSONS B&B		🛏 8
⏹	✂					🛏 7
		MIN £	MAX £	MIN £	MAX £	OPEN
		15.00	17.00	28.00	30.00	1-12

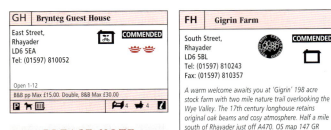

Monmouthshire and Brecon Canal, Talybont on Usk

Area
6

Ceredigion – Cardigan Bay

The southern arc of Cardigan Bay is dotted with pretty little ports and resorts, the largest of which is Victorian Aberystwyth with its splendid seafront. Long sections of this seashore have been designated Heritage Coast, including the exposed headland of Ynys Lochtyn near Llangrannog where on stormy days it almost seems as if you are sailing away from the mainland on board a ship. Inland, you'll discover traditional farming country matched by traditional country towns. Venture a little further and you'll come to the Cambrian Mountains, a compelling wilderness area crossed only by the occasional mountain road. The Teifi Valley, in contrast, is a gentle, leafy landscape famous for its beautiful river scenery, falls and coracle fishing.

Cenarth

It's a fact...

Dylan Thomas took much of his inspiration for the fictitious seatown of Llareggub in Under Milk Wood from New Quay. Remote Strata Florida Abbey, Pontrhydfendigaid, was known as the 'Westminster Abbey of Wales' in medieval times. Aberystwyth's Cliff Railway, opened in 1896, is Britain's longest electric-powered cliff railway. Cardigan Bay's bottlenose blue dolphin population is one of only two known to reside in UK coastal waters. The coracle, a tiny, one-man fishing boat used in Wales for 2000 years, can still be seen on the waters of the River Teifi.

Fc4 — Aberaeron

Most attractive little town on Cardigan Bay, with distinctive, Georgian-style architecture. Pleasant harbour, marine aquarium, coastal centre, courtyard craft workshops. Sailing popular, good touring centre for coast and country.

Fe2 — Aberystwyth

Premier resort on the Cardigan Bay coastline. Fine promenade, cliff railway, camera obscura, harbour and many other seaside attractions. Excellent museum in restored Edwardian theatre. University town, lively arts centre with theatre and concert hall. National Library of Wales stands commandingly on hillside. Good shopping. Vale of Rheidol narrow-gauge steam line runs to Devil's Bridge falls.

Fa5 — Cardigan

Market town on mouth of River Teifi close to beaches and resorts. Good shopping facilities, accommodation, inns. Golf and fishing. Base for exploring inland along wooded Teifi Valley and west to the Pembrokeshire Coast National Park. Y Felin Corn Mill and ruined abbey at neighbouring St Dogmael's. Welsh Wildlife Centre nearby.

Ga2 — Devil's Bridge

The spectacular Mynach Falls and Punchbowl make a glorious sight in a wooded gorge. A narrow-gauge steam railway runs here from Aberystwyth along the lovely Vale of Rheidol. Beautiful walks, nature trails, picnic sites abound.

Fe5 — Lampeter

Farmers and students mingle in this distinctive old market town in the picturesque Teifi Valley. Concerts are often held in St David's University College, and visitors are welcome. Golf and angling, range of small shops and some old inns. Visit the landscaped Cae Hir Gardens, Cribyn.

Fb4 — Llangrannog

Popular with children as a summer holiday beach, this is an ideal base for touring the Cardigan Bay coast - a typical little seaside village in very pretty setting. Dry ski slope at nearby Urdd Youth Camp. Take the spectacular coast walk to nearby Ynys Lochtyn headland.

Fc4 — New Quay

Picturesque little resort with old harbour on Cardigan Bay. Lovely beaches and coves around and about. Good for sailing and fishing. Resort sheltered by protective headland.

Fc4 — Oakford

Village tucked away in country lanes a few miles from Cardigan Bay coast; Aberaeron and New Quay nearby. Also a good touring centre for inland Ceredigion and the Teifi Valley.

Aberaeron

GH | Llys Alaw

Henfynyw,
Aberaeron
SA46 0EY
Tel: (01545) 570743

HIGHLY COMMENDED

Open 4-9
B&B Double £36.00 - £40.00

H | The Groves Hotel & Restaurant

North Parade,
Aberystwyth
SY23 2NF
Tel: (01970) 617623
Tel: (01970) 627068

COMMENDED

Open 1-12
B&B Double Min £50.00

H | Southgate Hotel

Antaron Avenue,
Penparcau
Aberystwyth
SY23 1SF
Tel: (01970) 611550

COMMENDED

Open 1-12
B&B pp Min £25.00. Double, B&B £40.00 - £50.00

GH | Meysydd

Rhiwgoch,
Ffosyffin,
Aberaeron
SA46 0EY
Tel: (01545) 571486

HIGHLY COMMENDED

Quiet location with private parking near Aberaeron. Comfortable, immaculate twin and double en-suite rooms. Completely non-smoking, guests TV lounge. Ideal base for exploring beautiful coast and countryside of Mid Wales.

		SINGLE PER PERSON B&B		DOUBLE FOR 2 PERSONS B&B		
		MIN £	MAX £	MIN £	MAX £	OPEN
		–	–	32.00	40.00	4-9

🛏 2 🛏 2

H | Marine Hotel

Marine Terrace,
Promenade,
Aberystwyth SY23 2BX
Tel: (01970) 612444
Fax: (01970) 617435

COMMENDED

Seafront family-run hotel with lift to all floors. Newly refurbished, spectacular sea views, de luxe suites, jacuzzi, steam shower, four poster. Traditional Welsh cuisine, grills and home-cooked bar meals. Conference facilities 10-350. Christmas/New Year breaks. Disabled facilties and bedroom. Ideal for touring North and South Wales. Car parking. TV, tea making. Special weekly rate available.

		SINGLE PER PERSON B&B		DOUBLE FOR 2 PERSONS B&B		
		MIN £	MAX £	MIN £	MAX £	OPEN
		25.00	25.00	50.00	50.00	1-12

🛏 35 🛏 33

GH | Pantgwyn

Llanfarian,
Aberystwyth
SY23 4DE
Tel: (01970) 612031

COMMENDED

This family-run guest house is situated in rural countryside in its own five acres of grounds on the A487 just outside the village of Llanfarian. Private parking, all rooms have hot and cold, tea/coffee making facilities, central heating, colour TV, some rooms en-suite.

		SINGLE PER PERSON B&B		DOUBLE FOR 2 PERSONS B&B		
		MIN £	MAX £	MIN £	MAX £	OPEN
		16.00	21.00	32.00	42.00	1-12

🛏 3 🛏 2

GH | Glyn-Garth Guest House

South Road,
Aberystwyth
SY23 1JS
Tel: (01970) 615050

HIGHLY COMMENDED

Situated adjacent to south promenade near harbour and castle. This highly recommended guest house has been run by the Evans family for over forty years. Excellent accommodation and food. Totally non-smoking. Most rooms en-suite some with side seaview, colour TV, tea/coffee facilities. Lock up garages available. A warm welcome always. AAQQQQ, RAC Highly Acclaimed. SAE for colour brochure.

		SINGLE PER PERSON B&B		DOUBLE FOR 2 PERSONS B&B		
		MIN £	MAX £	MIN £	MAX £	OPEN
		19.00	–	36.00	50.00	1-12

🛏 10 🛏 6

Call in at a Tourist Information Centre

Wales network of TIC's helps you get the best out of your holiday
• Information on what to see and where to go
• Local events
• Bed-booking service
• Brochures, maps and guides

It's so easy when you call in at a TIC

FGH | Y Gelli

Lovesgrove,
Aberystwyth
SY23 3HP
Tel: (01970) 617834

HIGHLY COMMENDED

Open 1-12
B&B pp £15.00 - £20.00. Double, B&B £30.00 - £40.00

🛏 5 🛏 2

FH | Tycam Farm

Capel Bangor,
Abeystwyth
SY23 3NA
Tel: (01970) 880662

COMMENDED

Peaceful dairy and sheep farm in glorious Rheidol Valley 7.5 miles Aberystwyth, 2.5 miles off A 44. Real home comforts are offered in traditional Cardiganshire farmhouse. Lounge, dining room, separate tables, colour TV. Perfect walking, birdwatching, sightseeing half a mile. Superb salmon, sewin, trout fishing on farm plus nearby lakes. Golf.

		SINGLE PER PERSON B&B		DOUBLE FOR 2 PERSONS B&B		
		MIN £	MAX £	MIN £	MAX £	OPEN
		–	–	36.00	38.00	2-11

🛏 2 🛏 2

WALES CYMRU
TWO HOURS AND A MILLION MILES AWAY

Cardigan Devil's Bridge Lampeter Llangrannog Oakford

FGH | Brynhyfryd Guest House

Gwbert Road,
Cardigan
SA43 1AE
Tel: (01239) 612861
Fax: (01239) 612861

HIGHLY COMMENDED

Long established guest house where a warm welcome and a high standard of comfort, cleanliness and good food is always assured. Situated in a pleasant part of Cardigan, two miles picturesque Cardigan Bay - home of dolphins. Bedrooms have colour TV, clock radio, hairdryer, tea/coffee facilities and comfortable beds. AA/RAC Recommended. Easy parking, fire certificate. Nesta and Ieuan Davies.

		SINGLE PER PERSON B&B		DOUBLE FOR 2 PERSONS B&B		🛏 6
		MIN £	MAX £	MIN £	MAX £	OPEN
		16.50	17.00	33.00	37.00	1-12

H | Dyffryn Castell Hotel

Ponterwyd,
Nr Devils Bridge,
Aberystwyth
SY23 3LB
Tel: (01970) 890237
Fax: (01970) 890237

COMMENDED

Ideally situated in the tranquil Cambrian Mountains for exploring the attractions of Mid Wales by car. Fishing, walking, birdwatching – Red Kite area – golf and pony trekking. Bars and restaurant are renowned for good food, beer and wine. Mostly en-suite bedrooms with colour TV, beverage facilities. Reduction for children. Come and experience a true Welsh welcome in the hillside.

		SINGLE PER PERSON B&B		DOUBLE FOR 2 PERSONS B&B		🛏 9
		MIN £	MAX £	MIN £	MAX £	OPEN
		25.00	25.00	40.00	50.00	1-12

FGH | Brynog Mansion

Felinfach,
Lampeter
SA48 8AQ
Tel: (01570) 470266

HIGHLY COMMENDED

Secluded spacious 250 year old country mansion and 170 acre grazing farm, approached by three quarters of a mile rhododendron lined drive off the A482. Fifteen minutes by car, Lampeter University town and seaside resort of Aberaeron and coast. Full Welsh breakfast in the grand old dining room. Rough shooting, birdwatching, riverside walks. Brochure available. Open all year round except Chistmas and New Year.

		SINGLE PER PERSON B&B		DOUBLE FOR 2 PERSONS B&B		🛏 3
		MIN £	MAX £	MIN £	MAX £	OPEN
		18.50	19.00	36.00	38.00	1-12

FGH | Pantycelyn Farm Guest House

Llanwnnen,
Lampeter
SA48 7LW
Tel: (01570) 434455

HIGHLY COMMENDED

Relax at Pantycelyn, a comfortable farmhouse in peaceful unspoilt countryside 5 miles west of Lampeter, within easy reach of Cardigan Bay, Teifi Valley and Cambrian Mountains. Ideal base for enjoying Ceredigion's abundant attractions. En-suite bedrooms, lounge with television, genuine home cooking, ample local information and the Nantgwinau Welsh Cobs and foals.

		SINGLE PER PERSON B&B		DOUBLE FOR 2 PERSONS B&B		🛏 3
		MIN £	MAX £	MIN £	MAX £	OPEN
		16.00	19.00	32.00	38.00	1-12

FH | Penlanmedd

Llanfair Road,
Lampeter
SA48 8JZ
Tel: (01570) 493438

HIGHLY COMMENDED

Open 1-12

B&B pp £22.00 - £24.00. Double, B&B £34.00 - £38.00

🅿 🛏 🍽 🛏 3 🛏 3

GH | Berry Green Guest House

Blaencelyn,
Nr Llangrannog
SA44 6DE
Tel: (01239) 654678
Fax: (01239) 654678

HIGHLY COMMENDED

Open 3-10

B&B pp £18.00 - £22.00. Double, B&B £36.00 - £40.00

🅿 🐾 🅲 🍽 🛏 2 🛏 2

FGH | Parc

Oakford,
Nr Llanarth
SA47 0RX
Tel: (01545) 580390

AWAITING GRADING

Traditional 17th century farmhouse, pleasant location in picturesque village three miles Aberaeron, New Quay. Friendly family atmosphere, three bedrooms, two with wash-hand basins, tea making facilities. Full central heating, colour TV, sunlounge. Pleasant garden for relaxation. Ideal for walking, birdwatching. Overlooking trout pools, many delightful bays and coves nearby. Ideal base for touring.

		SINGLE PER PERSON B&B		DOUBLE FOR 2 PERSONS B&B		🛏 3
		MIN £	MAX £	MIN £	MAX £	OPEN
		14.00	16.00	28.00	32.00	1-12

Aberystwyth

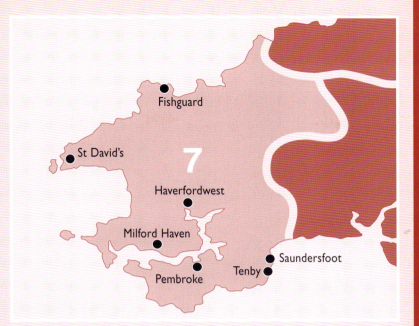

Fishguard

St David's

7

Haverfordwest

Milford Haven

Pembroke

Tenby

Saundersfoot

Pembrokeshire is traditionally known as *gwlad hud a lledrith*, 'the land of magic and enchantment'. Anyone who has visited the sandy bays around Tenby, for example, or the breathtaking sea-cliffs at Stack Rocks, or the rugged coastline around St David's will agree with this description. Pembrokeshire is one of Europe's finest stretches of coastal natural beauty. Not surprisingly, it's also a haven for wildlife. Wildflowers grow on its cliffs, seals swim in its clear waters, and seabirds nest in huge numbers all along the coast.

Pembrokeshire's stunning coastal beauty extends inland to the Preseli Hills, an open expanse of highland scattered with mysterious prehistoric sites. And away from the coast you'll also discover castles and a host of places to visit.

Stack Rocks

It's a fact...

The Pembrokeshire Coast National Park, created in 1952, covers 225 square miles from Poppit Sands in the north to Amroth in the south. The park's symbol is the razorbill, a reflection of the prolific seabird populations to be found here. The Pembrokeshire Coast Path, opened in 1970, runs for 186 miles. The Dale Peninsula is the sunniest place in Wales. The last invasion of British soil took place at Carreg Wastad beach near Fishguard in 1797 when a French force was soon seen off by the locals.

Pembrokeshire – Britain's
Only Coastal National Park

PEMBROKESHIRE - BRITAIN'S ONLY COASTAL NATIONAL PARK

Jb5 — Broad Haven

Sand and green hills cradle this holiday village on St Bride's Bay in the Pembrokeshire Coast National Park. Beautiful beach and coastal walks. National Park Information Centre.

Jb5 — Little Haven

Combines with Broad Haven - just over the headland - to form a complete family seaside holiday centre in the Pembrokeshire Coast National Park. The village dips down to a pretty sandy beach. Popular spot for sailing, swimming and surfing.

Jb3 — Croes-goch

Small village, useful spot for touring Pembrokeshire Coast National Park - especially its peaceful, rugged northern shores and nearby centres of St David's and Fishguard. Llangloffan Farmhouse Cheese Centre nearby.

Jb5 — Marloes

Village near Marloes Sands, a remote stretch of the Pembrokeshire Coast National Park - and one of its finest beaches - overlooking Skomer Island, a haven for puffins and other seabirds. Boat trips to the island from nearby Martin's Haven.

Jc2 — Fishguard

Lower Fishguard is a cluster of old wharves and cottages around a beautiful sheltered harbour. Shopping in Fishguard town. Good walks along Pembrokeshire Coast Path and in the country. Nearby Goodwick is the Irish ferry terminal, with a direct link from London. Excellent range of craft workshops in area including Tregwynt Woollen Mill. Music Festival in July.

Jc6 — Milford Haven

Important port on edge of Pembrokeshire Coast National Park; Nelson called it one of the best natural harbours he had seen. Marina in redeveloped docks has maritime museum and other attractions. Fine walks and gardens. Torch Theatre and leisure centre. Excellent touring base.

Jd2 — Newport

Ancient castled village on North Pembrokeshire coast. Fine beaches - bass and sea trout fishing. Pentre Ifan Burial Chamber is close by. Backed by heather-clad Preseli Hills and overlooked by Carn Ingli Iron Age Fort.

Jd6 — Freshwater East

Sheltered sandy bay South-east of Pembroke backed by dunes. Good beach, access for boats, limited car parking.

Jd6 — Pembroke

Ancient borough built around Pembroke Castle, birthplace of Henry VII. In addition to its impressive castle, well-preserved sections of old town walls. Fascinating Museum of the Home. Sandy bays within easy reach, yachting, fishing - all the coastal activities associated with estuaries. Plenty of things to see and do in the area, including visit to beautiful Upton Castle Grounds.

Jc5 — Haverfordwest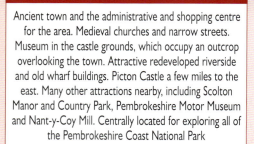

Ancient town and the administrative and shopping centre for the area. Medieval churches and narrow streets. Museum in the castle grounds, which occupy an outcrop overlooking the town. Attractive redeveloped riverside and old wharf buildings. Picton Castle a few miles to the east. Many other attractions nearby, including Scolton Manor and Country Park, Pembrokeshire Motor Museum and Nant-y-Coy Mill. Centrally located for exploring all of the Pembrokeshire Coast National Park

Ja4 St David's

Smallest cathedral city in Britain, shrine of Wales's patron saint. Magnificent ruins of a Bishop's Palace beside ancient cathedral nestling in hollow. Set in Pembrokeshire Coast National Park, with fine beaches nearby; superb scenery on nearby headland. Craft shops, sea life centres, painting courses, boat trips to Ramsey Island, farm park; ideal for walking and birdwatching.

Jb6 Sandy Haven

Hamlet west of Milford Haven near the entrance to the sheltered waters of the Haven. Overlooks inlet of Sandyhaven Pill. Promontory of Great Castle Head to the south.

Je6 Saundersfoot

Very attractive resort and sailing centre on the South Pembrokeshire coast within the national park. Good sandy beach and pretty harbour filled with colourful holiday craft. Excellent sea fishing. Tenby and a host of places to visit nearby, including Folly Farm, a family attraction based at a large working farm.

Jb4 Solva

Pretty Pembrokeshire coast village with small perfectly sheltered harbour and excellent craft shops. Pembrokeshire Coast Path offers good walking. Famous cathedral at nearby St David's.

Je6 Tenby

Popular, picturesque South Pembrokeshire resort with two wide beaches. Fishing trips from the attractive Georgian harbour and boat trips to nearby Caldy Island. The medieval walled town has a maze of charming narrow streets and fine old buildings, including Tudor Merchant's House (National Trust). Galleries and craft shops, excellent museum on headland, good range of amenities. Attractions include Manor House Leisure Park and 'Silent World' Aquarium. Wales in Bloom winner 1997.

Ka2 Whitland

Small market town close to the vast sandy beaches of Carmarthen Bay. Hywel Dda Gardens recall the work of an influential Welsh leader. Two popular attractions nearby - Grove Land Adventure World and Pemberton's Victorian Chocolates.

Saundersfoot Harbour (top)

St David's Cathedral

Broad Haven Croes-goch Fishguard Freshwater East

GH Lion Rock

Haroldston Hill,
Broad Haven
SA62 3JP
Tel: (01437) 781645
Tel: (01437) 781203

COMMENDED
GOLD

Cliff top position with stunning views over St Brides Bay. One minute walk to coastal path, three minutes walk to safe, sandy beach, watersports available nearby. Best beaches in Pembrokeshire all within easy reach. A warm welcome all year round. Ideal for long holidays and short breaks. Packed lunches available. Excellent breakfasts our speciality.

		SINGLE PER PERSON B&B		DOUBLE FOR 2 PERSONS B&B		🛏 5 🛏 5
		MIN £	MAX £	MIN £	MAX £	OPEN
		18.00	20.00	44.00	50.00	1-12

FGH The Bower Farm

Little Haven,
Haverfordwest
SA62 3TY
Tel: (01437) 781554

AWARD
HIGHLY COMMENDED
GOLD

Friendly working farmhouse with sheep, horses and poultry. Fantastic views over St Brides Bay and offshore islands. Walking distance of sandy beach and coast path. Run by local historic family who welcome long and short stay visitors, children and pets. Secluded, safe, peaceful, private, relaxing. Unrivalled recommendations. Fully en-suite with that 'something special feel'.

		SINGLE PER PERSON B&B		DOUBLE FOR 2 PERSONS B&B		🛏 5 🛏 5
		MIN £	MAX £	MIN £	MAX £	OPEN
		25.00	25.00	40.00	50.00	1-12

GH Dau-Wynt

Croes-goch,
Haverfordwest
SA62 5JN
Tel: (01348) 837922

COMMENDED

Near St David's. Ideal for country and coastal walking. Bed and breakfast, en-suite rooms with sea view, TV, tea/coffee making facilities. Non-smoking. Parking.

		SINGLE PER PERSON B&B		DOUBLE FOR 2 PERSONS B&B		🛏 2 🛏 2
		MIN £	MAX £	MIN £	MAX £	OPEN
		–	–	32.00	34.00	4-9

H Cartref Hotel

15-19 High Sreet,
Fishguard,
SA65 9AW
Tel: (01348) 872430
Fax: (01348) 872430

COMMENDED

Open 1-12

B&B pp Min £20.00. Double, B&B £40.00 - £48.00

🛏 12 🛏 6

H The Ferryboat Inn & Restaurant

St David's Road,
Goodwick,
Nr Fishguard SA64 0AA
Tel: (01348) 874747
Fax: (01348) 874747

COMMENDED

Open 1-12

B&B pp Max £19.50. Double, B&B Max £35.00

🛏 5 🛏 1

GH Glanmoy Lodge

Tref-Wrgi Road,
Goodwick,
Fishguard SA64 0JX
Tel: (01348) 874333
Fax: (01348) 875050 Mobile: (0467) 428500

HIGHLY COMMENDED
GOLD

One night free when booking seven. Secure parking. Enjoy a restful holiday with us. Private and peaceful, close to Pembrokeshire Coast National Park. Idyllic home from home setting in spacious grounds with abundant wildlife. All bedrooms en-suite, double, twin and family. All amenities. Tea/coffee always available. Choice of breakfast and times. Ferry and beaches one mile.

		SINGLE PER PERSON B&B		DOUBLE FOR 2 PERSONS B&B		🛏 3 🛏 3
		MIN £	MAX £	MIN £	MAX £	OPEN
		20.00	25.00	32.00	40.00	1-12

Welcome Host

Customer care is our top priority.
It's what our Welcome Host scheme is all about. Welcome Host badge and certificate holders are part of a tradition of friendliness. The Welcome Host programme, which is open to everyone from hotel staff to taxi drivers, places the emphasis on warm Welsh hospitality and first-class service.

GH Heathfield Mansion

Mathry Road
Letterston
SA62 5EG
Tel: (01348) 840263
Fax: (01348) 840263

HIGHLY COMMENDED
GOLD

Our Georgian country house in its tranquil setting of pastures and woodlands is the perfect place to relax and be spoilt. It is ideally situated to explore Pembrokeshire's treasures. Comfortable guest rooms with beautiful views over rolling countryside, good food and wines. Scenic coastal and hill walking, with fishing, horseriding nearby. Golf only one mile away. Angelika Rees.

		SINGLE PER PERSON B&B		DOUBLE FOR 2 PERSONS B&B		🛏 3 🛏 3
		MIN £	MAX £	MIN £	MAX £	OPEN
		–	25.00	36.00	40.00	3-10

GH Ivybridge

Drim Mill
Dyffryn
Goodwick
SA64 0FT
Tel: (01348) 875366/872623
Fax: (01348) 872338

HIGHLY COMMENDED

Situated down a leafy lane, Ivybridge waits to welcome you. Relax in our heated indoor pool, sit by the fire in our comfortable visitors lounge. All rooms are en-suite with colour TV and hot drinks facilities. Home-cooking, special diets catered for. Ample off road parking, licensed bar. Two minutes from ferry port. Telephone for brochure.

		SINGLE PER PERSON B&B		DOUBLE FOR 2 PERSONS B&B		🛏 11 🛏 11
		MIN £	MAX £	MIN £	MAX £	OPEN
		19.50	23.50	39.00	47.00	1-12

FGH East Trewent Farm

Freshwater East,
Pembroke
SA71 5LR
Tel: (01646) 672127

COMMENDED

Birds, flowers, fresh air in abundance. East Trewent Farm adjoins the coastal path. Beach 400 yards. Fishing and riding nearby. Ideal for those who love the outdoor life. Licensed bar. Evening meals and packed lunches by arrangement. This part of Pembrokeshire remains totally unspoilt.

		SINGLE PER PERSON B&B		DOUBLE FOR 2 PERSONS B&B		🛏 5 🛏 5
		MIN £	MAX £	MIN £	MAX £	OPEN
		16.50	16.50	33.00	43.00	1-12

Freshwater East Haverfordwest Marloes Milford Haven

GH Seahorses

Freshwater East,
Pembroke
SA71 5LA
Tel: (01646) 672405

COMMENDED

Superb view overlooking the sea and on the Pembrokeshire Coastal Path. Freshwater East sandy beach is half a mile and there are many more nearby. Ideal touring centre for the castles. Pembroke town is three miles and Tenby eight miles.

P	IIII.	SINGLE PER PERSON B&B		DOUBLE FOR 2 PERSONS B&B		🛏 2 🛁 –
		MIN £	MAX £	MIN £	MAX £	OPEN
		–	–	30.00	34.00	5-9

FGH The Fold

Cleddau Lodge,
Camrose,
Haverfordwest
SA62 6HY
Tel: (01437) 710640

HIGHLY COMMENDED

Converted 17th century farmhouse in secluded garden overlooking River Cleddau. Private fishing available. Central to Pembrokeshire coast six miles. Double room with wash-hand basin, private shower room with WC. Separate entrance. Homely welcome. Part of 50 acre estate with gardens, woodlands and river. Views of the Preseli Hills.

P	IIII.		SINGLE PER PERSON B&B		DOUBLE FOR 2 PERSONS B&B		🛏 1 🛁 1
			MIN £	MAX £	MIN £	MAX £	OPEN
			16.50	18.50	31.00	36.00	3-10

GH Foxdale Guest House

Glebe Lane,
Marloes,
Haverfordwest
SA62 3AY
Tel: (01646) 636243

GOLD

HIGHLY COMMENDED

Friendly and comfortable guest house fully licensed with guests TV lounge. Close to cliff path, Skomer, Skokholm, Grassholm bird islands, Marloes sands and spectacular scenery and flora. Ideal for walking, birdwatching, watersports in Dale and seal watching. Telephone for brochure.

P	🐕	SINGLE PER PERSON B&B		DOUBLE FOR 2 PERSONS B&B		🛏 4 🛁 2
♀	IIII.	MIN £	MAX £	MIN £	MAX £	OPEN
		22.00	25.00	32.00	40.00	1-12

GH Greenways Guest House

Shoals Hook Lane,
Haverfordwest
SA61 2XN
Tel: (01437) 762345
Mobile: (0378) 136578

HIGHLY COMMENDED

Comfortable family-run guest house in an outstanding peaceful setting, ideal for all seasons. Ideal location for touring Pembrokeshire. Close to golf course, ferry terminals, Oakwood Park, islands. Ground floor bedrooms, colour TV, service trays. En-suite available. Private parking. A quiet retreat home from home, find peace in our haven. Children and pets welcome.

P	🐕	SINGLE PER PERSON B&B		DOUBLE FOR 2 PERSONS B&B		🛏 4 🛁 3
C	IIII.	MIN £	MAX £	MIN £	MAX £	OPEN
♀	🍴	25.00	25.00	40.00	50.00	1-12

FH Knock Farm

Camrose,
Haverfordwest
SA62 6HW
Tel: (01437) 762208

HIGHLY COMMENDED

Our working dairy farm is peacefully situated in a scenic valley in central Pembrokeshire, ten minutes from Pembrokeshires sandy beaches and coastline walks, two miles from Haverfordwest. Ideally situated for fishing, horseriding, walking, golf. Tasty home cooking, homely atmosphere, pretty centrally heated bedrooms, tea/coffee facilities. Large family bedroom en-suite. Reductions children and senior citizens.

P	🐕	SINGLE PER PERSON B&B		DOUBLE FOR 2 PERSONS B&B		🛏 3 🛁 1
IIII.	🍴	MIN £	MAX £	MIN £	MAX £	OPEN
		15.00	17.50	30.00	35.00	3-11

H Beggars Reach Hotel

Burton,
Nr Milford Haven
SA73 1PD
Tel: (01646) 600700/600560

HIGHLY COMMENDED

Set in a very quiet position, this country house hotel is an ideal base for exploring Pembrokeshire. Once an early Victorian rectory now fully modernised, it has excellent guest rooms all with en-suite facilities, TV, telephone, coffee/tea. Restaurant and fully licensed bar. Full central heating. Ample car parking facilities.

P	🐕	SINGLE PER PERSON B&B		DOUBLE FOR 2 PERSONS B&B		🛏 10 🛁 9
C	♀	MIN £	MAX £	MIN £	MAX £	OPEN
IIII.	🍴	–	–	45.00	45.00	1-12

FH Cuckoo Mill Farm

Pelcomb Bridge,
St David's Road,
Haverfordwest
SA62 6EA
Tel: (01437) 762139

COMMENDED

Ideally situated peacefully in central Pembrokeshire on working family farm, two miles from Haverfordwest, ten minutes drive to coastline walks, sandy beaches, golf course, riding stables. Real home comfort in pretty well-appointed rooms. Excellent home-cooked meals. Reductions for senior citizens and children. Personal attention.

P	🐕	SINGLE PER PERSON B&B		DOUBLE FOR 2 PERSONS B&B		🛏 3 🛁 1
IIII.	🍴	MIN £	MAX £	MIN £	MAX £	OPEN
		15.00	17.50	30.00	35.00	1-12

H The Lobster Pot Inn & Restaurant

Marloes,
Haverfordwest
SA62 3AZ
Tel: (01646) 636233

COMMENDED

En-suite bedrooms with tea facilities, central heating, TV lounge, parking. Fifteen minutes walk to sandy beaches en-route Skomer, Grassholm, Skokholm bird islands. Suitable coastal path, walking, windsurfing, yachting, diving. Restaurant open to non-residents. Sunday lunches, teas, coffees, real ale, bar meals or full restaurant menu. Please write or phone for brochure.

P	♀	SINGLE PER PERSON B&B		DOUBLE FOR 2 PERSONS B&B		🛏 3 🛁 3
IIII.	♀	MIN £	MAX £	MIN £	MAX £	OPEN
	🍴	16.00	25.00	–	–	1-12

H The Ferry House Inn

Hazelbeach,
Milford Haven
SA73 1EG
Tel: (01646) 600270

COMMENDED

Just what you are looking for. Family-run inn set in picturesque village by the river, en-suite rooms, restaurant, real ales, popular with locals. Seasonal pontoon landing facility. Patio garden. Ideal central location for visiting beautiful Pembrokeshire. On route of coastal path. Close to Neyland marina and Pembroke Irish ferry port. Most major credit cards accepted.

P	🐕	SINGLE PER PERSON B&B		DOUBLE FOR 2 PERSONS B&B		🛏 6 🛁 6
♀	IIII.	MIN £	MAX £	MIN £	MAX £	OPEN
♀	🍴	17.00	20.00	30.00	40.00	1-12

Newport Pembroke St David's

GH | Grove Park Guest House

Pen-y-Bont Road,
Newport
SA42 0LT
Tel: (01239) 820122

GOLD

HIGHLY COMMENDED

Grove Park is situated on the outskirts of Newport, 100 yards from the Pembrokeshire Coastal Path. 19th century sea captains house which has been completely refurbished but retains original character. Estuary and mountain views, easy distance from large sandy beach and Preseli Mountains. Imaginative three course dinner menu. Winter breaks, log fires, hearty casseroles. Colour TV all bedrooms.

P	🐾	SINGLE PER PERSON B&B		DOUBLE FOR 2 PERSONS B&B		🛏 4
🍷	🛏					🚿 2
✕	🍽	MIN £ 24.00	MAX £ –	MIN £ 38.00	MAX £ 43.00	OPEN 1-12

GH | Springhill

2 Springhill,
Parrog Road,
Newport SA42 0RH
Tel: (01239) 820626

HIGHLY COMMENDED

Open 1-12

B&B pp Min £16.00. Double, B&B Min £32.00

P 🛏 🍽 | 🛏 3 🚿 – | ℹ

FH | Bangeston Farm

Stackpole,
Pembroke
SA71 5BX
Tel: (01646) 683986

GOLD

HIGHLY COMMENDED

Open 4-9

B&B pp Max £15.00. Double, B&B Max £30.00

P 🛏 | 🛏 4 🚿 – | ℹ

FH | Poyerston Farm

Cosheston,
Pembroke
SA72 4SJ
Tel: (01646) 651347
Fax: (01646) 651347

GOLD

HIGHLY COMMENDED

Open 3-10

B&B pp £19.00 - £21.00. Double, B&B £38.00 - £40.00

P 🛏 ✕ 🍽 | 🛏 5 🚿 5 | ℹ

GH | Awel-Môr Guest House

Penparc,
Trefin,
Nr St David's
SA62 5AG
Tel: (01348) 837865
Fax: (01348) 837865

DE LUXE

Luxury non-smoking accommodation. Magnificent views overlooking sea and Pembrokeshire National Park. Large bedrooms with soft chairs, TV, tea/coffee facilities. Delicious food from breakfast/dinner menu. Optional evening meal. Table licence. Free brochure available. 'Best guest house in Wales'. Tourist Board Hospitality Award. Map grid ref: sm845312.

P	🍷	SINGLE PER PERSON B&B		DOUBLE FOR 2 PERSONS B&B		🛏 3
🛏	✕					🚿 1
🍽		MIN £ 25.00	MAX £ 25.00	MIN £ 40.00	MAX £ 50.00	OPEN 4-10

GH | Y Glennydd Restaurant & Guest House

51 Nun Street,
St David's
SA62 6NU
Tel: (01437) 720576
Fax: (01437) 720184

COMMENDED

A comfortable Victorian town house with ten bedrooms all with central heating, hot and cold, teasmaids, colour TV, hairdryers etc. Most en-suite, a few with splendid views. We also offer a licensed restaurant, bar and lounge with friendly service. Ideal centre for walking, cycling and any outdoor activities.

C	🍷	SINGLE PER PERSON B&B		DOUBLE FOR 2 PERSONS B&B		🛏 10
🛏						🚿 8
🍽		MIN £ 16.50	MAX £ 25.00	MIN £ 33.00	MAX £ 40.00	OPEN 1-10

GH | 5 Millard Park

St David's,
SA62 6QH
Tel: (01437) 720700

HIGHLY COMMENDED

Open 3-10

B&B Double £36.00 - £37.00

P 🛏 ✕ | 🛏 2 🚿 2 | ℹ

GH | Penberi Cottage

Fachelich,
St David's
SA62 6QL
Tel: (01437) 720528
Fax: (01437) 720528

HIGHLY COMMENDED

Situated in a quiet hamlet midway between Solva and St David's only half a mile from the coastal path. Excellent self contained spacious ground floor twin room, en-suite bathroom, easy chairs, dining facilities, colour television, beverage making facilities and exclusive parking. Dinner available by prior arrangement.

P	🐾	SINGLE PER PERSON B&B		DOUBLE FOR 2 PERSONS B&B		🛏 1
🛏	✕					🚿 1
🍽		MIN £ –	MAX £ –	MIN £ 34.00	MAX £ 34.00	OPEN 2-11

FH | Torbant Farmhouse

Croes-goch,
Haverfordwest
SA62 5JN
Tel: (01348) 831276
Fax: (01348) 831276

COMMENDED

A warm welcome awaits you at Torbant, a peacefully situated farmhouse near St David's and the Pembrokeshire Coast National Park. Sea is one and half miles away with beautiful beaches, magnificent scenery. We have two en-suite bedrooms with TV and beverage trays. Our lounge is available all day and also a utility room for laundry and picnic preparation.

P	🛏	SINGLE PER PERSON B&B		DOUBLE FOR 2 PERSONS B&B		🛏 2
C	🍽					🚿 2
		MIN £ 19.00	MAX £ 20.00	MIN £ 38.00	MAX £ 40.00	OPEN 3-10

Cyclists and Walkers Welcome

Look out for the 'boot' and 'bike' symbols. They are displayed by places which have undertaken to provide features which cyclists and/or walkers always find welcome. These include drying facilities for wet clothes and boots, secure lockable area for bikes, availability of packed lunches and so on. You'll even be greeted with a welcoming cup of tea or coffee on arrival.

Sandy Haven Saundersfoot Solva Tenby

FH Skerryback

Sandy Haven,
St Ishmael's,
Haverfordwest
SA62 3DN
Tel: (01646) 636598
Fax: (01646) 636595

HIGHLY COMMENDED
AWARD

18th century farmhouse set in an attractive garden surrounded by farmland, and the coastal path on the doorstep. A haven for walkers and birdlovers. Home cooking, en-suite, central heating backed up by log fires on chilly evenings.

P	IIII.	SINGLE PER PERSON B&B		DOUBLE FOR 2 PERSONS B&B		2
	YOI					1
		MIN £	MAX £	MIN £	MAX £	OPEN
		18.00	–	36.00	–	3-11

GH Cliff House

Wogan Terrace,
Saundersfoot
SA69 9HA
Tel: (01834) 813931
E-mail: blackm@globalnet.co.uk

HIGHLY COMMENDED
GOLD

Quality – comfort – service - welcome - words our guests tell us really mean something at Cliff House. In the heart of the village one minute walk from the beach with outstanding sea and harbour views. Ideal base for relaxation, sporting holidays or exploring beautiful Pembrokeshire. Quality en-suite facilities in several rooms. Personal service from resident proprietors. Somewhere special.

		SINGLE PER PERSON B&B		DOUBLE FOR 2 PERSONS B&B		3
IIII.	YOI					3
		MIN £	MAX £	MIN £	MAX £	OPEN
		17.00	25.00	34.00	50.00	1-12

GH Pinewood

Cliff Road,
Wiseman's Bridge,
Nr Saundersfoot
SA67 8NU
Tel: (01834) 811082

HIGHLY COMMENDED
GOLD

Adjacent to Pembrokeshire Coastal Path, halfway between Saundersfoot and Amroth. Comfortable large dormer bungalow in peaceful, rural surroundings, 350 yards from the beach, lounge with sea view. Twin and double rooms are en-suite on the ground floor, with colour TV, tea/coffee facilities. Ideal for relaxing, sightseeing and walking. Brochure Mrs Gwen Grecian.

P	IIII.	SINGLE PER PERSON B&B		DOUBLE FOR 2 PERSONS B&B		2
						2
		MIN £	MAX £	MIN £	MAX £	OPEN
		17.50	17.50	35.00	35.00	4-10

GH The Valley

Valley Road,
Saundersfoot
SA69 9BX
Tel: (01834) 813153

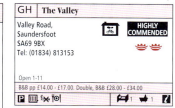

HIGHLY COMMENDED

Open 1-11

B&B pp £14.00 - £17.00. Double, B&B £28.00 - £34.00

P	IIII.		YOI		1	1

FGH Lochmeyler Farm Guest House

Pen-y-Cwm,
Nr Solva,
Haverfordwest
SA62 6LL
Tel: (01348) 837724
Fax: (01348) 837622

AWARD
GOLD

DE LUXE

Enjoy luxury accommodation on a working dairy farm. Non-smoking, en-suite bedrooms, some with four poster beds. All bedrooms have refreshment facilities, TV, video and Pembrokeshire information pack to help you explore the area. Home-cooking, daily choice of menus including vegetarian. Two lounges, one non-smoking. Children welcome. Colour brochure available. Major credit cards accepted.

P		SINGLE PER PERSON B&B		DOUBLE FOR 2 PERSONS B&B		12
	IIII.					12
	YOI	MIN £	MAX £	MIN £	MAX £	OPEN
		15.00	–	30.00	50.00	1-12

FH Olmarch Farm

Llandeloy,
Nr Solva,
Haverfordwest
SA62 6NB
Tel: (01348) 831247

COMMENDED

Open 3-10

B&B pp £13.50 - £15.50. Double, B&B £26.00 - £29.00

P		IIII.		YOI	3	1

H Clarence House Hotel

Esplanade,
Tenby
SA70 7DU
Tel: (01834) 844371
Fax: (01834) 844372

COMMENDED

Tenby town centre esplanade. South beach seafront.

Send for free colour brochure. Full information, discount tariff options. All you need to know.

		SINGLE PER PERSON B&B		DOUBLE FOR 2 PERSONS B&B		20
IIII.						20
	YOI	MIN £	MAX £	MIN £	MAX £	OPEN
		16.00	24.00	26.00	46.00	4-9

H Pen-Mar

New Hedges,
Tenby
SA70 8TL
Tel: (01834) 842435

HIGHLY COMMENDED

Open 1-12

B&B pp £17.50 - £23.50. Double, B&B £35.00 - £47.00

P		IIII.		YOI	10	6

Pets Welcome

You'll see from the symbols that many places to stay welcome dogs and pets by prior arrangement. Although some sections of beach may have restrictions, there are always adjacent areas - the promenade, for example, or quieter stretches of sands - where dogs can be exercised on and sometimes off leads. Please ask at a Tourist Information Centre.

Solva

57

Tenby Whitland

GH Flemish Court

St Florence,
Tenby
SA70 8LS
Tel: (01834) 871413
Fax: (01834) 871413

COMMENDED

Lovely home of June and Eric, where you will find a real Welsh welcome. All rooms en-suite. Sumptious breakfasts. All day access. Parking. Situated in floral village. Norman church opposite. Easy access to all attractions, coastal walks etc. Try us first for that restful relaxing holiday you all deserve. Evening meals available. Telephone June Taylor for brochure. Safe parking.

	SINGLE PER PERSON B&B		DOUBLE FOR 2 PERSONS B&B		🛏 3 🛏 3
	MIN £	MAX £	MIN £	MAX £	OPEN
	14.00	17.00	28.00	34.00	1-12

GH High Seas

8 The Norton,
Tenby
SA70 8AA
Tel: (01834) 843611
Fax: (01834) 843611

HIGHLY COMMENDED

This Georgian town house is in an ideal position with beautiful views of the beach and harbour. Close to town centre and only a few steps from the sands and safe bathing of the north beach. There are six bedrooms, five with private bathrooms, all have colour TV and tea/coffee making facilities.

	SINGLE PER PERSON B&B		DOUBLE FOR 2 PERSONS B&B		🛏 6 🛏 5
	MIN £	MAX £	MIN £	MAX £	OPEN
	18.00	24.00	32.00	44.00	4-10

FGH Landon Farm Guest House

Begelly,
Kilgetty
SA68 0NJ
Tel: (01834) 812164/811311

HIGHLY COMMENDED

Open 1-12

B&B pp Max £16.00. Double, B&B Max £28.00

🛏 3 🛏 3

H Weybourne Guest House

14 Warren Street,
Tenby
SA70 7JX
Tel: (01834) 843641

COMMENDED

Family run guest house with an informal atmosphere, central heating, double glazing. Close to railway station, bus station, town centre and beaches. All rooms have colour TV, tea/coffee facilities and radios. Contact Tracey or Tony for a brochure. Weekend breaks and midweek bookings accepted throughout the season.

	SINGLE PER PERSON B&B		DOUBLE FOR 2 PERSONS B&B		🛏 6 🛏 -
	MIN £	MAX £	MIN £	MAX £	OPEN
	13.00	15.00	26.00	30.00	2-10

PRICES

Single rates are for ONE PERSON in a single room. Double rates are for TWO PEOPLE sharing a double or twin room. There may be supplements for private bath/shower and single occupancy of a double/twin room. All prices include VAT. Please check all prices and facilities before confirming your booking.

FH Brunant

Whitland
SA34 0LX
Tel: (01994) 240421
Fax: (01994) 240421

HIGHLY COMMENDED

Welcome to our 200 year old farmhouse surrounded by attractive gardens and beautifully unspoilt countryside. Centrally situated for touring Pembrokeshire and Carmarthenshire. Well appointed bedrooms, all facilities. Details Mrs O Ebsworth.

	SINGLE PER PERSON B&B		DOUBLE FOR 2 PERSONS B&B		🛏 3 🛏 3
	MIN £	MAX £	MIN £	MAX £	OPEN
	18.00	20.00	36.00	40.00	4-9

FGH Cilpost Farm

Whitland
SA34 ORP
Tel: (01994) 240280

AWAITING GRADING

Ideally placed for touring Pembrokeshire, our 300 year old award-winning farmhouse is featured on the front cover of this book. Set amidst extensive lawns and gardens every modern amenity is provided including a magnificent indoor heated swimming pool and snooker room. Self-catering cottages are also available and you are warmly welcomed.

	SINGLE PER PERSON B&B		DOUBLE FOR 2 PERSONS B&B		🛏 7 🛏 4
	MIN £	MAX £	MIN £	MAX £	OPEN
	17.00	23.00	34.00	46.00	4-9

Tenby

Dylan Thomas captured the essence of this timeless part of Wales in his short stories and poems, but most of all in his masterwork, *Under Milk Wood*. Dylan lived at Laugharne, a sleepy seatown set amongst the sweeping sands of Carmarthen Bay. Here you can wander along endless beaches, and then turn your attention to the patchwork of green farmlands which roll gently down to the sea. There's a rare sense of peace and tranquillity in the countryside around Carmarthen. Explore the lovely Vale of Towy, the moors of Mynydd Llanybydder or the glades of the Brechfa Forest. And don't miss market day at Carmarthen, or the view from the ramparts of Carreg Cennen, one of Wales's most spectacular castles.

Dylan Thomas's Boathouse, Laugharne

It's a fact...

In the 1920s, the huge 6-mile beach at Pendine was used for land speed record attempts. Dolaucothi, Pumsaint, is the only place in Britain where we know, for certain, that the Romans mined for gold. The beach at Cefn Sidan, Pembrey, is 7 miles long. Twm Shôn Cati, Wales's answer to Robin Hood, hid in the hills north of Llandovery from the Sheriff of Carmarthen. Christmas mail can be postmarked from Bethlehem, a hamlet between Llandeilo and Llangadog.

CARMARTHENSHIRE - BEAUTIFUL COAST AND COUNTRYSIDE IN WEST WALES

Ke2   Ammanford

Bustling valley town, good for Welsh crafts and products, on western edge of Brecon Beacons National Park. Spectacular mountain routes over nearby Black Mountain to Llangadog.

Kc2   Carmarthen

Prosperous country town in pastoral Vale of Towy. Lively market and shops, livestock market. Carmarthen Castle was an important residence of the native Welsh princes but only the gateway and towers remain. Heritage Centre in riverside location. Golf, fishing, tennis and well-equipped leisure centre. Remains of Roman amphitheatre. Immaculate museum in beautiful historic house on outskirts of town. Gwili Railway nearby.

Ke2   Cross Hands

Town in rolling countryside south of Vale of Towy. Lots of places to visit nearby - Llyn Llech Owain Country Park, Paxton's Tower, castles. Also close to popular Pembrey Country Park and superb beach of Cefn Sidan.

Kc3   Kidwelly

Historic town 9 miles south of Carmarthen. Its first charter was granted by Henry I. With its ancient church, 14th-century bridge and great castle - one of the best preserved in Wales - it has a medieval air. Industrial museum on outskirts. Located on Gwendraeth Estuary, the town is close to Cefn Sidan Sands and Pembrey Country Park.

Gb6   Llandovery

An important market town on the A40 with a ruined castle, good craft shops and excellent local museum/information centre; its Welsh name Llanymddyfri means 'the church among the waters'. In the hills to the north is the cave of Twm Siôn Cati - the Welsh Robin Hood. Good touring centre for Brecon Beacons and remote Llyn Brianne area.

Ke2   Llandybie

Town between Ammanford and Llandeilo on western approach to Brecon Beacons National Park. Brooding Black Mountain and romantic Carreg Cennen Castle nearby. Much to see and do locally - country parks, historic sites, market towns.

Kb2   St Clear's

Good base for coast and country. Dylan Thomas's Laugharne and the huge beach at Pendine are to the south, with Carmarthenshire's rural heartlands to the north. Grove Land Adventure World a popular family attraction.

Llynne Brianne

CARMARTHENSHIRE - BEAUTIFUL COAST AND COUNTRYSIDE IN WEST WALES

Ammanford Carmarthen Cross Hands Kidwelly

GH Mount Pleasant

Pontardulais Road,
Garnswllt,
Ammanford
SA18 2RT
Tel: (01269) 591722
Fax: (01269) 591722

COMMENDED

Open 1-12

B&B pp £18.00 - £20.00. Double, B&B £32.00 - £36.00

GH Brynderwen

School Lane,
Llangain
SA33 5AE
Tel: (01267) 241403

HIGHLY COMMENDED

Open 4-9

B&B pp £17.50 - £20.00. Double, B&B £35.00 - £40.00

GH Y Dderwen Fach

98 Priory Street,
Carmarthen
SA31 1NU
Tel: (01267) 234193
Fax: (01267) 235766

COMMENDED

Open 1-12

B&B pp £14.00 - £19.50. Double, B&B £28.00 - £34.00

GH Glasfryn Guest House & Restaurant

Brechfa,
Carmarthen
SA32 7QY
Tel: (01267) 202306
Fax: (01267) 202306

HIGHLY COMMENDED

Family-owned friendly guest house situated in the beautiful village of Brechfa on the edge of the Brechfa Forest. Ideally situated for touring South West and Mid Wales. Twenty minutes from Carmarthen, 1 1/4 hours Fishguard ferry. Licensed conservatory restaurant, excellent home-cooked food, à la carte menu. All rooms en-suite. Ideal for walking, birdwatching, biking. Phone for brochure.

		SINGLE PER PERSON B&B	DOUBLE FOR 2 PERSONS B&B	🛏 3 🛏 3
		MIN £	MAX £	MIN £	MAX £	OPEN
		20.00	24.00	40.00	48.00	1-12

PLEASE NOTE

All accommodation in this publication has applied for grading. However, at the time of going to press not all establishments had been visited - some of these properties are indicated by the wording
'AWAITING GRADING'

FH Plas Farmhouse

Llangynog
SA33 5DB
Tel: (01267) 211492

COMMENDED
GOLD

Plas has been run by the Thomas family for almost a century. Situated just 5 miles west of Carmarthen along the A40 towards St Clears. Ideal touring base, one hours drive from Fishguard/Pembroke ferry to Ireland. Spacious farmhouse, en-suite available, tea/coffee tray. Full central heating. Good pubs nearby for evening meals. Ample parking. Enquiries Mrs Margaret Thomas.

		SINGLE PER PERSON B&B	DOUBLE FOR 2 PERSONS B&B	🛏 3 🛏 2
		MIN £	MAX £	MIN £	MAX £	OPEN
		20.00	25.00	32.00	36.00	1-12

FH Trebersed Farm

St Peters,
Travellers Rest,
Carmarthen
SA31 3RR
Tel: (01267) 238182
Fax: (01267) 223633

HIGHLY COMMENDED
AWARD
GOLD

Open 1-12

B&B pp Max £20.00. Double, B&B Max £36.00

GH Deangate Lodge

Black Lion Road,
Gorlas,
Cross Hands, Llanelli
SA14 6RU
Tel: (01269) 831900

HIGHLY COMMENDED

Open 1-12

B&B pp Max £25.00. Double, B&B £32.00 - £38.00

FH Ffynnon Rhosfa Farm

Llwynteg,
Llannon,
Llanelli
SA14 8JN
Tel: (01269) 845874
Fax: (01269) 831500

COMMENDED

Enjoy the tranquil settings of a tastefully refurbished farmhouse close to M4. Ideal stopover for Ireland and touring Carmarthen, Swansea, The Gower, Llanelli coast, Pembrey Park, Black Mountains. Offering a variety of facilities and attractions. Fishing, golfing, riding arranged. Discounts full/half board on application.

		SINGLE PER PERSON B&B	DOUBLE FOR 2 PERSONS B&B	🛏 4 🛏 4
		MIN £	MAX £	MIN £	MAX £	OPEN
		15.00	18.00	30.00	35.00	1-12

FGH Penlan Isaf Farm

Kidwelly,
SA17 5JR
Tel: (01554) 890084
Fax: (01554) 891191

DE LUXE
GOLD

Penlan Isaf overlooks the historical town of Kidwelly, with superb views of the countryside and Gower. Pembrey Park and Motor Museum centre three miles. Penlan is a 250 acre dairy farm. With modern spacious farmhouse, en-suite, colour TV all bedrooms, superb sun lounge. A warm welcome and excellent home-cooking awaits visitors. Great centre for touring mountains and the coast.

		SINGLE PER PERSON B&B	DOUBLE FOR 2 PERSONS B&B	🛏 3 🛏 3
		MIN £	MAX £	MIN £	MAX £	OPEN
		20.00	20.00	34.00	36.00	1-11

Gwili narrow-gauge Railway

61

Llandovery Llandybie St Clear's

FH | Cwmgwyn Farm

Llangadog Road,
Llandovery
SA20 0EQ
Tel: (01550) 720410
Fax: (01550) 720262

HIGHLY COMMENDED

Warm welcome to enjoy the country on our livestock farm overlooking the River Towy, two miles from Llandovery on A4069. The 17th century farmhouse is full of charm and character with inglenook fireplace, exposed stonework and beams. Spacious luxury en-suite bedrooms with hairdryer, colour TV, tea/coffee. Ideally situated for touring Mid and South Wales.

P	IIII.	SINGLE PER PERSON B&B		DOUBLE FOR 2 PERSONS B&B		🛏 3 🛏 3
		MIN £ 23.00	MAX £ 23.00	MIN £ 40.00	MAX £ 40.00	OPEN 4-10

GH | Glynhir Estate

Glynhir Mansion,
Llandybie
SA18 2TD
Tel: (01269) 850438/851461
Fax: (01269) 851275

COMMENDED

GOLD

18th century estate of character. Mansion house with large bedrooms, two en-suite. Relaxed, informal atmosphere, sitting room for guests own use. Idyllic parkland setting, 30ft waterfall in grounds. Excellent home-cooking using the freshest local produce. Variety of activities within seven mile radius, golfing, fishing, fly and course, riding and many beautiful walks and cycle rides.

P ♟ IIII. ⬥ 🍴		SINGLE PER PERSON B&B		DOUBLE FOR 2 PERSONS B&B		🛏 4 🛏 2
		MIN £ 16.50	MAX £ 25.00	MIN £ 33.00	MAX £ 50.00	OPEN 2-11

FH | Coed Llys Uchaf

Llangynin,
St Clears
SA33 4JY
Tel: (01994) 231455

AWAITING GRADING

Relax in the peaceful atmosphere of our farmhouse with beautiful views. Children enjoy helping us with the animals. Large comfortable bedrooms. Seven miles Dylan Thomas Laugharne, many beautiful beaches, castles and golf etc. a short drive. Lots to do in South West Wales. Afternoon tea served on arrival in guest lounge.

P 🐕		SINGLE PER PERSON B&B		DOUBLE FOR 2 PERSONS B&B		🛏 2 🛏 1
C IIII.						
✂ 🍴		MIN £ 17.50	MAX £ 20.00	MIN £ 35.00	MAX £ 40.00	OPEN 1-11

GH | Westwood House

Llanddowror,
St Clear's
SA33 4HL
Tel: (01994) 230512

HIGHLY COMMENDED

Open 4-10

B&B pp Max £20.00. Double, B&B Max £36.00

P IIII.	🛏3 🛏

Carreg Cennen Castle

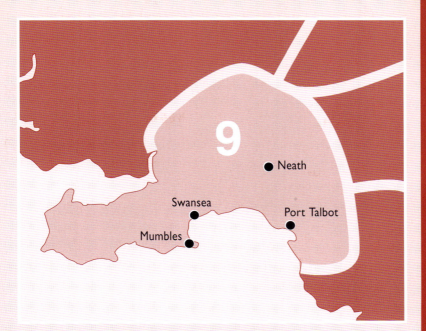

9

Neath

Swansea

Port Talbot

Mumbles

The city of Swansea enjoys a wonderful location. It stands on the grand curve of Swansea Bay at the doorstep to the beautiful Gower Peninsula and green Neath and Afan valleys. It's a maritime city through and through – there's even a stylish Maritime Quarter complete with marina and attractive waterside developments. Modern and traditional Wales mix happily in this friendly city. At its heart is a fresh foods market where you can buy welshcakes, laverbread and cockles from Penclawdd on Gower. The pretty little sailing centre of Mumbles stands at the gateway to Gower, a lovely peninsula with a string of sandy, south-facing bays and a towering curtain of cliffs. Inland, there are the forests and waterfalls of the Afan Valley and Vale of Neath to explore.

Swansea Market

It's a fact...

In 1956, the Gower Peninsula was the first part of Britain to be declared an 'Area of Outstanding Natural Beauty'. Swansea Museum, Wales's oldest museum, dates from the 1830s. The inaugural meeting of the Welsh Rugby Union was held at Neath in 1881. The waterwheel at the National Trust's Aberdulais Falls is Europe's largest electricity-generating waterwheel. The traditional Welsh delicacy known as laverbread (a kind of puréed seaweed) is usually eaten as an accompaniment to bacon and eggs.

Naturally Beautiful – Swansea Bay including Mumbles, Gower, the Afan Valley and Vale of Neath

NATURALLY BEAUTIFUL - SWANSEA BAY INCLUDING MUMBLES, GOWER, THE AFAN VALLEY AND VALE OF NEATH

La4 Mumbles

Small resort on Swansea Bay with attractive waterfront and headland pier; centre for watersports and sailing. On fringe of Gower Peninsula, a designated 'Area of Outstanding Natural Beauty'. Oystermouth Castle and Clyne Valley Country Park and Gardens nearby.

Kd5 Oxwich

Popular Gower Peninsula beach with 3 miles of glorious sand and extensive dunes; easily accessible. Nature trail and visitor centre.

Kd5 Port Eynon

An old smugglers' haunt on Gower. Pretty crescent of sands a popular spot in summer. Westwards there's a spectacular walk along a remote stretch of cliffs to Rhossili. Culver Hole on headland is a local oddity.

Kd5 Reynoldston

Gower Peninsula village near the sandy beaches of Oxwich, Port-Eynon and Rhossili.

Ke5 Southgate

Gower Peninsula village; fine beaches at Three Cliffs Bay and Oxwich, and popular Caswell and Langland bays just to the east. Close to Swansea with its leisure centre, Maritime Quarter, museums and shopping.

La4 Swansea

Wales's second city and gateway to the Gower Peninsula, Britain's first designated 'Area of Outstanding Natural Beauty'. Superb modern marina complex and Maritime Quarter - excellent leisure centre, with Maritime and Industrial Museum alongside. Art gallery, Dylan Thomas Centre at Ty Llên, Superbowl, dry ski slope and marvellous 'Plantasia' exotic plants attraction. Good shopping. Covered market with distinctively Welsh atmosphere: try the cockles, laverbread and Gower potatoes. Swansea Festival and 'Fringe' Festival in October. Theatres and cinemas, parks and gardens, restaurants and wine bars.

Swansea Marina (top)

Cliffs near Pennard, Gower Peninsular

64

Mumbles   Oxwich   Port Eynon   Reynoldston   Southgate   Swansea

---

GH | The Coast House

708 Mumbles Road,
Mumbles
SA3 4EH
Tel: (01792) 368702

HIGHLY COMMENDED

Family run guest house. Seafront location with magnificent views of Swansea Bay. All rooms (except single en-suite) have good sea views, colour TV, tea making facilities, radio/alarms and hairdryers. Most rooms are en-suite. Local amenities include golf, horseriding, sandy beaches, cliff walking. Swansea University, Swansea/Cork ferry four miles. RAC Acclaimed.

		SINGLE PER PERSON B&B		DOUBLE FOR 2 PERSONS B&B			6
							4
		MIN £	MAX £	MIN £	MAX £	OPEN	
		18.00	20.00	34.00	38.00	1-12	

GH | Little Haven Guest House

Oxwich,
Gower
SA3 1LS
Tel: (01792) 390940

COMMENDED

We are a family-run guest house. All rooms have hot and cold and tea/coffee making facilities. Family room en-suite with TV. We are close to the beach which is ideal for most watersports with many coastal walks. We have a secluded garden where your can relax and have a picnic.

		SINGLE PER PERSON B&B		DOUBLE FOR 2 PERSONS B&B			4
							1
		MIN £	MAX £	MIN £	MAX £	OPEN	
		19.00	19.00	34.00	34.00	1-12	

GH | Langford

Port Eynon,
Gower
SA3 1NL
Tel: (01792) 390365

HIGHLY COMMENDED

Open 1-12

B&B pp Max £18.00. Double, B&B Max £34.00

		3
		-

FGH | Greenways Hills Farm

Reynoldston,
Gower
SA3 1AE
Tel: (01792) 390125

COMMENDED

Open 2-11

B&B pp £15.00 - £20.00. Double, B&B £30.00 - £38.00

			3
			-

FGH | Sunnyside

Llanddewi Castle Farm,
Llanddewi,
Reynoldston
SA3 1AU
Tel: (01792) 390194

COMMENDED

Open 1-11

B&B pp Min £16.00. Double, B&B Min £32.00

		2
		-

GH | Headlands

28A East Cliff,
Southgate
SA3 2AS
Tel: (01792) 234208

HIGHLY COMMENDED

Open 1-12

B&B pp £16.00 - £16.00. Double, B&B £32.00 - £32.00

		3
		-

GH | Heatherlands

1 Hael Lane,
Southgate,
Gower
SA3 2AP
Tel: (01792) 233256

HIGHLY COMMENDED

Delightfully situated Heatherlands is an immaculate residence, secluded garden, near cliffs and sea. Short walk Pobbles and Three Cliffs Bay. Bedrooms with hot and cold, shaver points and tea/coffee facilities. One bedroom en-suite, two bedrooms private bathrooms. TV lounge, separate tables in dining room, excellent breakfast, warm welcome. Meals available in local pub and restaurants.

		SINGLE PER PERSON B&B		DOUBLE FOR 2 PERSONS B&B			3
							1
		MIN £	MAX £	MIN £	MAX £	OPEN	
		21.00	23.00	36.00	40.00	1-11	

H | Cefn Bryn Hotel

6 Uplands Cresent,
Swansea
SA2 0PB
Tel: (01792) 466687

HIGHLY COMMENDED

Open 1-12

B&B pp Max £25.00. Double, B&B Max £42.00

		7
		7

GH | Richmond Villa

55 Overland Road
Mumbles
Swansea
SA3 4EU
Tel: (01792) 367813

COMMENDED

We are in the heart of Mumbles, the house pre-Victorian style and 100 yards from the promenade, water sports and shops. We are six miles from Swansea centre, maritime quarter and leisure centre. Easy access to the beautiful Gower bays. Very comfortable rooms with sea views. All rooms have TV and refreshment facilities.

		SINGLE PER PERSON B&B		DOUBLE FOR 2 PERSONS B&B			3
							-
		MIN £	MAX £	MIN £	MAX £	OPEN	
		17.00	17.00	34.00	34.00	1-12	

PRICES

Single rates are for ONE PERSON in a single room. Double rates are for TWO PEOPLE sharing a double or twin room. There may be supplements for private bath/shower and single occupancy of a double/twin room. All prices include VAT. Please check all prices and facilities before confirming your booking.

Rhossili

65

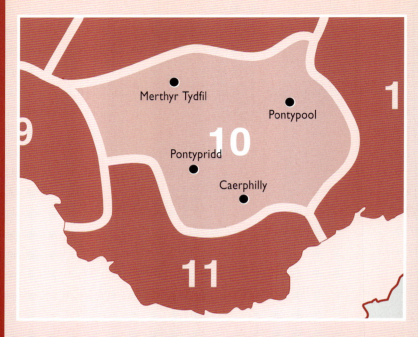

Merthyr Tydfil

Pontypool

10

Pontypridd

Caerphilly

1

9

11

The Valleys of South Wales

The Valleys of South Wales are full of surprises – dramatic natural beauty, country and wildlife parks, forest and cycle trails, and a huge range of attractions. Did you know that Caerphilly Castle is regarded as one of Europe's greatest surviving examples of medieval military architecture? Or that there's a scenic narrow-gauge railway which takes you into the foothills of the Brecon Beacons from Merthyr Tydfil? Or that you can enjoy everything from walking to watersports at an exceptional range of country parks? Yet the past hasn't been entirely forgotten. Although the Valleys are green again, there's a rich industrial heritage at places like the Big Pit Mining Museum, Blaenavon, and the Rhondda Heritage Park, Trehafod.

Brecon Mountain Railway

It's a fact...

Caerphilly Castle, which covers 12 hectares/30 acres, is one of Britain's largest. Its 'leaning tower' out-leans Pisa's. In the 19th century, Merthyr Tydfil was Wales's largest town and the 'iron capital of the world'. The world's first steam engine, built by Cornishman Richard Trevithick, ran from Merthyr to Abercynon in 1804. There are around 15 country parks in the Valleys. Pontypridd is singer Tom Jones's home town. Blaenavon's Big Pit Mining Museum was a working colliery until 1980. The last coalmine in the Rhondda closed at the end of 1990.

Mb3 Blackwood

Southern valley town surrounded by pine-clad hills rising to mountain tops. Visit Penyfan Pond, a country park a few miles to the north, attractive Parc Cwm Darran and the Sirhowy Valley Country Park. Tour Llancaiach Fawr historic house and Stuart Crystal's glass factory nearby.

Ma4 Caerphilly

A sight not to be missed - 13th-century Caerphilly Castle is one of Europe's finest surviving medieval strongholds and has a famous leaning tower. Golf course, shopping, good centre for exploring the Valleys and visiting Cardiff. Fine views and pleasant walks from Caerphilly Mountain.

Mc3 Cwmbran

A 'new town' development and administrative centre. Good leisure facilities. Llantarnam Grange Arts Centre. Shopping and sports centre with international athletics stadium. Theatre and cinemas. Well-located touring centre for the Vale of Usk and South Wales Valleys.

Ma4 Nelson

Small town between Taff and Rhymney valleys. Open mountains to north and south. Nearby Llancaiach Fawr manor house one of the most impressive historic sites in the Valleys.

Mc3 Pontypool

Historic metal-producing town on eastern edge of South Wales Valleys. Attractive park contains Valley Inheritance heritage centre and long dry ski slope. Big Pit Mining Museum and rurally located Llandegfedd Reservoir both nearby.

Big Pit, Blaenafon (top)

Caerphilly Castle

Blackwood Caerphilly Cwmbran Nelson Pontypool

GH | Wyrloed Lodge

Manmoel
Blackwood
NP2 0RW
Tel: (01495) 371198
Fax: (01495) 243322

COMMENDED

Victorian style house all en-suite with TV, beverage trays. Situated in village with pub, church, playing field and park. Ideal for touring Cardiff and Brecon areas. Excellent for walking holidays.

P 🐕 📺	SINGLE PER PERSON B&B		DOUBLE FOR 2 PERSONS B&B		🛏 3 🍽 3
	MIN £	MAX £	MIN £	MAX £	OPEN
	18.00	20.00	36.00	36.00	1-12

GH | Springfields Guest House

371 Llantarnam Road,
Llantarnam,
Cwmbran NP44 3BN
Tel: (01633) 482509

COMMENDED

Hope to celebrate 25 years at Springfields this year. 'Enjoying the company of many more pleasant guests and then they pay me! We are ideally situated 5 minutes from M4, 45 minutes to M50. Pleasant area, semi-rural and close to so many attractions in this lovely area of South East Wales. Hope you'll visit. Thanks Joan and Graham.

P 🐕 📺	SINGLE PER PERSON B&B		DOUBLE FOR 2 PERSONS B&B		🛏 9 🍽 6
	MIN £	MAX £	MIN £	MAX £	OPEN
	17.00	20.00	33.00	37.00	1-12

FGH | Mill Farm

Cwmafon,
Torfaen
NP4 8XJ
Tel: (01495) 774588

HIGHLY COMMENDED

15th century farmhouse in idyllic setting, experience complete tranquillity in en-suite bedrooms individually furnished with antiques. Central heating throughout. Enjoy breakfast until noon, logfires, oak beams, four poster bedroom, spiral staircases. Swim in our indoor heated pool situated in the lounge. Barbecue in the garden. Explore the woodlands. Ideal centre for walking, touring or visiting attractions.

P C 📺	SINGLE PER PERSON B&B		DOUBLE FOR 2 PERSONS B&B		🛏 4 🍽 4
	MIN £	MAX £	MIN £	MAX £	OPEN
	25.00	25.00	40.00	50.00	1-12

GH | Monterey Guest House

23 Coed Leddyn,
Caerphilly
CF83 2NF
Tel: (01222) 882633
Fax: (01222) 882633

HIGHLY COMMENDED

Situated in one and half acres of grounds with nature corner, farmland and forestry walks to the rear. Newly refurbished. Excellent food, good conversation with that warm friendly feeling. A delightful place to stay. Panoramic views over Caerphilly Castle and town centre, yet minutes walk from good restaurants, sports leisure and shopping complexes.

P C 📺	SINGLE PER PERSON B&B		DOUBLE FOR 2 PERSONS B&B		🛏 3 🍽 3
	MIN £	MAX £	MIN £	MAX £	OPEN
	24.90	24.90	39.00	39.00	1-12

GH | Fairmead Guest House

24 Gelligaer Road,
Nelson
CF46 6DN
Tel: (01443) 411174
Fax: (01443) 411174

HIGHLY COMMENDED

Open 1-12

B&B pp £22.50 - £25.00. Double, B&B £45.00 - £50.00

P 🐕 C 📺 ✕ 🍽 | 🛏 3 🍽 3

FGH | Wern Ganol Farm

Nelson
CF46 6PS
Tel: (01443) 450413

HIGHLY COMMENDED

Wern Ganol is a 60 acre dairy farm on the main A472 at Nelson with pleasant views over the surrounding countryside. Near to Llancaiach Fawr Manor House and Caerphilly Castle, also Brecon Beacons, Cardiff and the South Wales coast. Junction 32 M4 twenty minutes.

P 🐕 📺	SINGLE PER PERSON B&B		DOUBLE FOR 2 PERSONS B&B		🛏 6 🍽 6
	MIN £	MAX £	MIN £	MAX £	OPEN
	18.00	25.00	36.00	38.00	1-12

Prices

In this publication we go to great lengths to make sure that you have a clear, accurate idea of prices and facilities. It's all spelled out in the 'Prices' section - and remember to confirm everything when making your booking.

Llancaiach Fawr

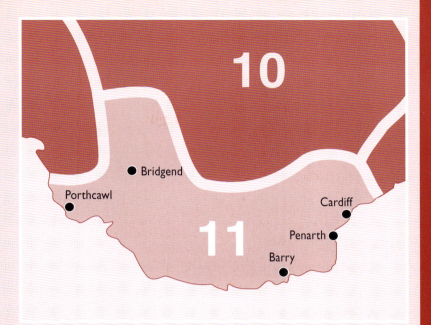

10

● Bridgend

Porthcawl
●

11

Cardiff
●

Penarth ●

Barry
●

Cardiff is Wales's cosmopolitan capital city. It's a place of culture and the arts, with fine museums and theatres. It's also a city of great style – Cardiff's neoclassical civic architecture has won praise worldwide while the lavish city-centre castle, a seriously Victorian creation, never fails to astonish. The castle was built with the wealth generated by Cardiff's booming 19th-century seaport. The city is now renewing its maritime links through the exciting Cardiff Bay development, which is transforming the old waterfront. Close to the city there's attractive coast and countryside. The pastoral Vale of Glamorgan is dotted with picturesque villages and thatched cottages. And along the shore there's everything from the spectacular cliffs of the Glamorgan Heritage Coast to the popular resorts of Barry Island and Porthcawl.

Civic Centre, Cardiff

It's a fact...

Cardiff was declared capital city of Wales in 1955. The Cardiff Bay development will create 8 miles of new waterfront and a 202-hectare/500-acre freshwater lake. In 1999 the city plays host to the Rugby World Cup. Cardiff is only two hours by train from London. Cardiff-born author Roald Dahl was baptised in the city's Norwegian Church. The Glamorgan Heritage Coast, designated in 1973, runs for 14 miles between Aberthaw and Porthcawl. Merthyr Mawr has the highest sand dunes in Britain, rising to over 61m/200ft. Ewenny, near Bridgend, boasts Wales's oldest working pottery.

Cardiff and the
Glamorgan Heritage Coast

Mb5 Cardiff

Capital of Wales, business, trade and entertainment centre. Splendid Civic Centre, lovely parkland, modern pedestrianised shopping centre, new waterfront development, good restaurants, theatres, cinemas, clubs and sports facilities, including ice-rink and Superbowl. Visit St David's Hall and International Arena for top-class entertainment. Ornate city-centre castle. National Museum and Gallery has a fine collection of Impressionist paintings. Industrial and Maritime Museum and Techniquest science discovery centre on Cardiff Bay waterfront. New Millennium Stadium, replacing the famed Arms Park, opens 1999. Llandaff Cathedral close by as well as fascinating collection of old farmhouses and other buildings at the Museum of Welsh Life, St Fagans. City was Wales in Bloom winner 1997.

Le6 Cowbridge

Picturesque town with wide main street and pretty houses - the centre of the Vale of Glamorgan farming community. Fine old inns, shops selling high-class clothes and country wares. Fourteenth-century town walls. Good touring centre for South Wales. Visit nearby Beaupre Castle.

Lc6 Porthcawl

Traditional seaside resort - beaches, funfair, promenade. Attractive harbour and quieter coast along Rest Bay. Summer entertainment at the Grand Pavilion. Sailing and windsurfing. Famous golf course. Kenfig Pool and Dunes. Convenient for visiting unspoilt South Wales countryside - Bryngarw Country Park and Vale of Glamorgan with its attractive villages set amid leafy lanes.

Norwegian Church, Cardiff Bay

H Wynford Hotel

Clare Street,
Cardiff, CF1 8SD
Tel: (01222) 371983
Fax: (01222) 340477

COMMENDED

Very close to the city centre, train and bus stations. The Wynford, privately owned and personally supervised, offers a comfortable lounge, two cosy bars, occasional music and dancing, bistro and restaurant. All rooms have colour TV and telephone. Many have private bathroom. French, German and Spanish spoken. Night porter. Video linked security car park.

P ¥ 🛏 🍴		SINGLE PER PERSON B&B		DOUBLE FOR 2 PERSONS B&B		🛏 20 🛏 18
		MIN £	MAX £	MIN £	MAX £	OPEN
		25.00	25.00	40.00	50.00	1-12

H Austins

11 Coldstream Terrace,
Cardiff
CF1 8LJ
Tel: (01222) 377148
Fax: (01222) 377158

COMMENDED

Small friendly family-run hotel 300 metres from Cardiff Castle, overlooking the River Taff. All city centre attractions are within a few minutes walk. Cardiff central station is 10 minutes walk along the river. All rooms have tea/coffee and colour TV. En-suite rooms available. A warm welcome offered to all nationalities. Come and enjoy Cardiff this year.

🐕 C 🛏	SINGLE PER PERSON B&B		DOUBLE FOR 2 PERSONS B&B		🛏 11 🛏 4
	MIN £	MAX £	MIN £	MAX £	OPEN
	16.00	24.00	30.00	35.00	1-12

GH Farthings

Lisvane Road,
Lisvane,
Cardiff
CF4 5SG
Tel: (01222) 756404

HIGHLY COMMENDED

Close to Cardiff centre yet in the heart of the village of Lisvane, Farthings offers single and double cottage style accommodation with private bathroom and lounge, plus secure parking. A few minutes walk from local inn serving meals. Close to bus and rail services to city centre and beyond.

P 🛏 🕯✗	SINGLE PER PERSON B&B		DOUBLE FOR 2 PERSONS B&B		🛏 2 🛏
	MIN £	MAX £	MIN £	MAX £	OPEN
	25.00	25.00	38.00	38.00	1-12

GH Plas-y-Bryn

93 Fairwater Road,
Llandaff
Cardiff. CF5 2LG
Tel: (01222) 561717

HIGHLY COMMENDED

Open 1-12

B&B pp £17.00 - £25.00. Double, B&B £32.00 - £50.00

🐕 🛏 🕯✗ 🛏 3 🛏 ℹ

CA The Welsh Institute of Sport

Sophia Gardens,
Cardiff
CF1 9SW
Tel: (01222) 300500
Fax: (01222) 300600

APPROVED

Set in attractive parklands location in the centre of Cardiff only ten minutes walk from the train and bus stations, the Institute offers an extensive range of services. Residents are able to enjoy the superb sporting facilities including a swimming pool, health suite, gym, tennis, badminton and much more.

P ¥ 🛏 🍴		SINGLE PER PERSON B&B		DOUBLE FOR 2 PERSONS B&B		🛏 30 🛏 30
		MIN £	MAX £	MIN £	MAX £	OPEN
		19.80	24.15	–	–	1-12

GH Crossways House

Cowbridge
CF71 7LJ
Tel: (01446) 773171
Fax: (01446) 773171

HIGHLY COMMENDED

GOLD

The vales best kept secret! A friendly rural family home with excellent facilities. Discerning guests will appreciate this beautiful historic mansion with impressive turret, barrel-vaulted ceiling and wood panelling. In a tranquil setting of six acres of mature grounds with tennis court, lawns, woods, home produced eggs and honey. Convenient Cardiff, coast and M4.

P 🐕 🛏 🕯✗	SINGLE PER PERSON B&B		DOUBLE FOR 2 PERSONS B&B		🛏 3 🛏 3
	MIN £	MAX £	MIN £	MAX £	OPEN
	25.00	–	50.00	50.00	1-12

H Penoyre

29 St Mary Street,
Porthcawl
CF36 3YN
Tel: (01656) 784550

COMMENDED

Penoyre is a family-run hotel 100 yards from beach and shopping centre. All rooms have colour TV, tea/coffee making facilities, en-suite available. Small friendly bar and TV lounge with satellite TV provided for guests enjoyment. Children and pets welcome. Excellent home-cooking, vegetarian and special diets on request. A la carte menu. RAC Acclaimed.

🐕 ¥ 🛏 🍴		SINGLE PER PERSON B&B		DOUBLE FOR 2 PERSONS B&B		🛏 7 🛏 4
		MIN £	MAX £	MIN £	MAX £	OPEN
		16.00	20.00	32.00	38.00	1-12

GH Rockybank Guest House

15 De Breos Drive,
Porthcawl
CF36 3JP
Tel: (01656) 785823
Fax: (01656) 785823

HIGHLY COMMENDED

Open 1-12

B&B pp £24.00 - £26.00. Double, B&B £40.00 - £44.00

P 🛏 🕯 🛏 2 🛏 2 ℹ

WALES ON THE
WEB

Make the most of your visit to Wales by calling into the NEW Wales Tourist Board site from mid-January 1998. It's your easy route to up-to-date information on accommodation, attractions and events in Wales, as well as ideas for itineraries and themes to explore. Just dial into 'Wales on the Web' at:

www.tourism.wales.gov.uk

WALES CYMRU
TWO HOURS AND A MILLION MILES AWAY

Wye Valley and Vale of Usk

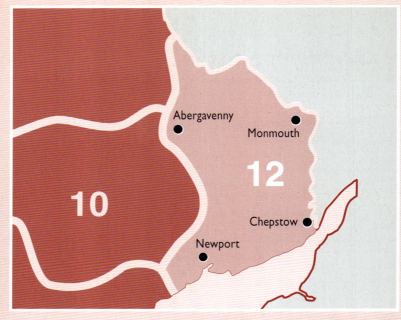

Abergavenny

Monmouth

12

10

Chepstow

Newport

These two lovely valleys, close to the border, serve as the best possible introduction to Wales. The thickly wooded Wye Valley snakes its way northwards from Chepstow through countryside which is beautiful in all seasons. It's a walker's paradise, with a wonderful choice of trails including woodland, riverside and Offa's Dyke paths. Rolling green hills separate the Wye from the Usk, another beautiful river valley which reaches the sea at Newport. Fishermen, as well as walkers, love this part of Wales, for both rivers are famed for their salmon and trout. These borderlands, a natural gateway into Wales over the centuries, are dotted with historic sites of great significance – the Roman town of Caerleon, castles at almost every turn, and the splendid 17th-century mansion of Tredegar House, Newport.

River Usk

It's a fact...

The Wye Valley between Chepstow and Monmouth is an 'Area of Outstanding Natural Beauty', designated in 1971. Among the Wye Valley's earliest tourists was poet William Wordsworth, who was inspired to write Lines Composed a Few Miles Above Tintern Abbey in 1798. Britain's first stone-built castle was constructed at Chepstow in 1067. Charles Stewart Rolls, of Rolls-Royce celebrity, is a famous son of Monmouth – his statue stands in the town square. The Skirrid Inn at Llanfihangel Crucorney near Abergavenny is reputed to be the oldest pub in Wales.

Mc1 Abergavenny

Flourishing market town with backdrop of mountains at south-eastern gateway to Brecon Beacons National Park. Pony trekking in nearby Black Mountains. Castle and museum. Leisure centre. Monmouthshire and Brecon Canal runs just to the west of the town. Excellent touring base for the lovely Vale of Usk and Brecon Beacons.

Me4 Caerwent

This village between Newport and Chepstow was once the Roman town of Venta Silurum. Long sections of a Roman perimeter walls remain together with an excavated temple. Nearby Wentwood Forest has attractive walks. Penhow Castle also close by.

Me4 Chepstow

Attractive hilly town with substantial remains of a great stone castle - reputedly the first to be built in Britain - above the Wye. Fortified gate still stands in main street and medieval walls remain. Good shopping. Museum, Stuart Crystal Engraving Workshop. Sunday market, fine racecourse, excellent walks - beginning of the Wye Valley Walk and Offa's Dyke Path. Ideal for touring beautiful Wye Valley.

Me1 Monmouth

Historic market town in picturesque Wye Valley - birthplace of Henry V and Charles Rolls (of Rolls-Royce). Interesting local history museum with collection of Nelson memorabilia. Rare fortified gateway still spans the River Monnow. Ruined castle close to town centre. Well located for touring Wye Valley and borderland Wales.

Mc4 Newport

Busy industrial, commercial and shopping centre. Interesting murals in main hall of Civic Centre. Newport Museum and Art Gallery in John Frost Square (named after Chartist leader) and leisure centre with wave machine. On the outskirts, magnificently restored Tredegar House set in extensive grounds, and 14 Locks Canal Visitor Centre. St Woolos Cathedral on hill overlooking town centre. Ruined castle on riverside near shops and attractive Victorian market hall.

Mc3 Pontypool

Historic metal-producing town on eastern edge of South Wales Valleys. Attractive park contains Valley Inheritance heritage centre and long dry ski slope. Big Pit Mining Museum and rurally located Llandegfedd Reservoir both nearby.

Md2 Raglan

Historic village dominated by Raglan Castle, noted for its impressive Great Tower of Gwent. Convenient for touring the Usk and Wye valleys and eastern Brecon Beacons. Wales in Bloom winner 1997.

Mc5 St Brides Wentloog

Settlement on mouth of Usk close to Newport overlooking Severn Estuary. Splendid Tredegar House nearby; Cardiff only a short distance away.

Me3 Tintern

Riverside village in particularly lovely stretch of Wye Valley. Impressive ruins of Tintern Abbey not to be missed. The former railway station has a visitors' interpretive centre and picnic site with refreshments. Excellent walks and good fishing.

Abergavenny

H	Black Lion Hotel

Lion Street,
Abergavenny
NP7 5PE
Tel: (01873) 853993

APPROVED

Friendly Welsh family-run tavern, nice clean accommodation, tea/coffee facilities, TV, bar meals, roast lunches available all day. A whole range of outdoor activities on the doorstep, fishing, hiking, pony trekking. Seven mountains surrounding the town, hang gliding is also available. A lovely canal on the outskirts of the town.

P	🐴	SINGLE PER PERSON B&B		DOUBLE FOR 2 PERSONS B&B		🛏 3
C	🍴					–
🏠	🍽	MIN £	MAX £	MIN £	MAX £	OPEN
		17.50	18.00	32.00	35.00	1-12

H	Kings Head Hotel

Cross Street,
Abergavenny
NP7 5EU
Tel: (01873) 853575

COMMENDED

The Kings Head is a 16th century coaching inn situated in the centre of Abergavenny. An ideal base for exploring the Black Mountains, Brecon Beacons and castles. Enjoy a relaxing stay with us in comfortable surroundings with the very best in home cookery and a well kept hostelry. All rooms en-suite with TV and hostess trays.

P	🍴	SINGLE PER PERSON B&B		DOUBLE FOR 2 PERSONS B&B		🛏 6
🏠	🍽					6
		MIN £	MAX £	MIN £	MAX £	OPEN
		25.00	25.00	40.00	45.00	1-12

H	The Lancaster Arms

Old Hereford Road,
Pandy,
Nr Abergavenny
NP7 8DW
Tel: (01873) 890699
Fax: (01873) 890699
Open 1-12

COMMENDED

B&B pp £18.00 - £20.00. Double, B&B £32.00 - £35.00

P	🐴	🍴	🏠	🍽		🛏 2	1

GH	Brook Cottage

Llanvetherine,
Nr Abergavenny
NP7 8RG
Tel: (01873) 821315

HIGHLY COMMENDED

Open 1-11

B&B pp £16.50 - £25.00. Double, B&B £25.00 - £33.00

🐴	🏠	🍽			🛏 2	–	

GH	Heathfield

Nant-y-Derry,
Abergavenny
NP7 9DP
Tel: (01873) 880675

GOLD

HIGHLY COMMENDED

AWARD

Country house set in a large garden with a croquet lawn, views of the Blorenge Mountain. Comfortable and spacious rooms, all centrally heated with tea/coffee lounge, TV lounge. Good inns and restaurants just five minutes walk away. Five miles from Abergavenny, four miles from Usk. Walks in peaceful countryside, excellent golf courses two miles away.

P	🏠	SINGLE PER PERSON B&B		DOUBLE FOR 2 PERSONS B&B		🛏 3
🍴						1
		MIN £	MAX £	MIN £	MAX £	OPEN
		–	–	34.00	40.00	3-11

GH	The Old Rectory

Llangattock-Lingoed,
Nr Abergavenny
NP7 8RR
Tel: (01873) 821326

HIGHLY COMMENDED

Situated in an acre of mature gardens amidst the rolling hills. Local facilities include pony trekking, fishing, sailing, golf, hang gliding, caving, walking. Places of interest in surrounding areas, Brecon Beacons, Black mountain ranges, Llanthony Priory, Tintern Abbey and many castles. Guest lounge with TV, evening meals optional.

P	🏠	SINGLE PER PERSON B&B		DOUBLE FOR 2 PERSONS B&B		🛏 4
🍽						–
		MIN £	MAX £	MIN £	MAX £	OPEN
		17.00	17.00	34.00	34.00	1-12

GH	Park Guest House

36 Hereford Road,
Abergavenny
NP7 5RA
Tel: (01873) 853715

COMMENDED

Attractive detached Georgian guest house, close to town centre. All rooms with hand basins, beverage trays, TV, and radio. Two bathrooms, lounge, dining room with separate tables. High quality four course evening meals available by arrangement. Fully licensed. Free private parking. Convenient for Brecon Beacons, 'Big Pit', castles and museums. Detailed brochure on request.

P	C	SINGLE PER PERSON B&B		DOUBLE FOR 2 PERSONS B&B		🛏 7
🍴	🏠					–
⚡	🍽	MIN £	MAX £	MIN £	MAX £	OPEN
		18.00	20.00	32.00	36.00	1-12

GH	Pentre House

Brecon Road,
Abergavenny
NP7 7EW
Tel: (01873) 853435
Fax: (01873) 853434

AWARD

HIGHLY COMMENDED

Small pretty country house situated at the turning for Sugar Loaf mountain A40 to Brecon. Set in one acre of award-winning gardens. Bathroom and shower room, sitting room with woodburner. Very comfortably furnished, peaceful surroundings, River Usk just down lane, pony trekking, golf and excellent walks. Evening meals. Brochure on request.

P	🐴	SINGLE PER PERSON B&B		DOUBLE FOR 2 PERSONS B&B		🛏 3
🏠	⚡					–
	🍽	MIN £	MAX £	MIN £	MAX £	OPEN
		18.00	25.00	32.00	38.00	1-12

FH	High House Farm

Bryngwyn,
Raglan
NP5 2BS
Tel: (01291) 690529
Fax: (01291) 690529

HIGHLY COMMENDED

Open 4-10

B&B pp £18.00 - £20.00. Double, B&B £36.00 - £40.00

P	🐴	🏠			🛏 3	1	

The Complete Guides to South Mid and North Wales

In full colour and packed with information - a must for all visitors. Fully revised and redesigned in a new format for 1998

• Where to go and what to see •
Descriptions of towns, villages & resorts
• Hundreds of attractions & places to visit
• Detailed maps and town plans

• Scenic drives, beaches, narrow-gauge railways, what to do on a rainy day

£5.40 each inc. p&p

(see 'Guides and Maps' at the end of the book)

H | Coach and Horses Inn

Caerwent,
Nr Newport
NP6 4AX
Tel: (01291) 420352
Fax: (01291) 424491

COMMENDED

Friendly village pub set amid beautiful countryside on the site of the Roman town of Venta Salurum, visit the Roman city of Caerleon or Tintern Abbey in the Wye Valley. A short journey to one of four local golf courses including the famous St Pierre golf club near Chepstow. Traditional home-cooked food.

	SINGLE PER PERSON B&B		DOUBLE FOR 2 PERSONS B&B		🛏 3 🛌 3
	MIN £	MAX £	MIN £	MAX £	OPEN
	25.00	30.00	35.00	40.00	1-12

GH | Oakhill Lodge

Hewelsfield
Lydney
GL15 6UN
Tel: (01594) 530261
Te: (01594) 530261

DE LUXE
GOLD

Overlooking River Severn and the Cotswolds, Wye Valley two miles. Our beautiful secluded family home in three acres of gardens and 34 acres of adjoining woodland and walks offers relaxing luxury ground floor accommodation all en-suite. Licensed, evening meals available, indoor heated swimming pool. Easy access to M4. Your satisfaction is Roger and Gwendolens aim.

	SINGLE PER PERSON B&B		DOUBLE FOR 2 PERSONS B&B		🛏 3 🛌 3
	MIN £	MAX £	MIN £	MAX £	OPEN
	18.00	18.00	36.00	36.00	3-10

F | Sunnybank Farm

Devauden,
Nr Chepstow
NP6 6NS
Tel: (01291) 650365

HIGHLY COMMENDED
GOLD

A homely welcome awaits you in our refurbished farmhouse on working farm. Double and twin rooms all en-suite with TV, tea/coffee facilities, relaxing guest lounge with TV, inglenook dining room. Ideal for touring Usk and Wye Valleys, Royal Forest of Dean. Enjoy our unspoilt countryside visiting castles, walking, golf, fishing or racing at Chepstow.

	SINGLE PER PERSON B&B		DOUBLE FOR 2 PERSONS B&B		🛏 3 🛌 3
	MIN £	MAX £	MIN £	MAX £	OPEN
	18.00	19.00	34.00	36.00	3-12

GH | Church Farm Guest House

Mitchel Troy,
Monmouth
NP5 4HZ
Tel: (01600) 712176

COMMENDED

A spacious and homely 16th century former farmhouse with oak beams and inglenook fireplaces. Set in large attractive garden with stream. Easy access to A40 and only two miles from historic Monmouth. Excellent base for Wye Valley, Forest of Dean and Black Mountains. Large car park. Terrace, barbecue. Colour TV, central heating, tea/coffee making facilities.

	SINGLE PER PERSON B&B		DOUBLE FOR 2 PERSONS B&B		🛏 8 🛌 6
	MIN £	MAX £	MIN £	MAX £	OPEN
	18.00	21.00	36.00	42.00	1-12

GH | Scatterford Cottage

The Butts,
Clearwell
GL16 8PW
Tel: (01594) 835527

COMMENDED

Detached modern cottage in one and half acres overlooking open country on edge of village well situated for Royal Forest of Dean and Wye Valley. Rooms with television and tea making, separate bathroom with shower and bath. Separate toilet. Own parking. Approximately six miles from Monmouth.

	SINGLE PER PERSON B&B		DOUBLE FOR 2 PERSONS B&B		🛏 2 🛌 -
	MIN £	MAX £	MIN £	MAX £	OPEN
	18.00	20.00	30.00	34.00	1-12

FH | New House Farm

Dingestow,
Monmouth
NP5 4EB
Tel: (01600) 740245
Fax: (01600) 740245

COMMENDED

Open 1-12

B&B pp £17.00 - £19.00. Double, B&B £34.00 - £38.00

🅿 🛏 🍴🗙 🍽 🛏 3 🛌 -

FH | Pentre-Tai Farm

Rhiwderin,
Newport
NP1 9RQ
Tel: (01633) 893284
Fax: (01633) 893284

HIGHLY COMMENDED

Open 2-11

B&B pp £22.00 - £23.00. Double, B&B £34.00 - £38.00

🅿 🛏 🍴🗙 🛏 3 🛌 2

GH | Bluetts Houses Bed & Breakfast

2 Bluetts Houses,
Bluetts Lane, Victoria Village,
Pontypool
NP4 7AP
Tel: (01495) 774445/774600
Fax: (01495) 774600

HIGHLY COMMENDED

Picturesque rural location below historical viaduct. Large wildlife pond in garden. TV, hospitality trays in rooms. Central for walking and numerous tourist attractions. Fishing and field sports by arrangement. We will make your visit as comfortable as possible - a real Welsh welcome, home from home.

	SINGLE PER PERSON B&B		DOUBLE FOR 2 PERSONS B&B		🛏 3 🛌 -
	MIN £	MAX £	MIN £	MAX £	OPEN
	-	21.00	-	34.00	1-12

FGH | Brooklands Farm

Chepstow Road,
Raglan
NP5 2EN
Tel: (01291) 690782
Mobile: (0850) 635314

COMMENDED

Working dairy farm with sheep and cattle. Situated close to Raglan Castle and within 200 metres of Raglan Village with its shops and pubs. Large spacious garden, local golf course, walking, fishing, horseriding all within a short distance. Ideal touring centre.

	SINGLE PER PERSON B&B		DOUBLE FOR 2 PERSONS B&B		🛏 4 🛌 1
	MIN £	MAX £	MIN £	MAX £	OPEN
	15.00	18.00	30.00	36.00	1-12

Welcome Host

Customer care is our top priority.
It's what our Welcome Host scheme is all about. Welcome Host badge and certificate holders are part of a tradition of friendliness. The Welcome Host programme, which is open to everyone from hotel staff to taxi drivers, places the emphasis on warm Welsh hospitality and first-class service.

St Brides Wentloog Tintern

GH	Chapel Guest House

COMMENDED

Church Road,
St Brides Wentloog
NP1 9SN
Tel: (01633) 681018
Fax: (01633) 270470

Comfortable en-suite accommodation in a converted chapel situated in village between Newport and Cardiff. Inn/restaurant adjacent, pleasant walks, fishing, golf, Tredegar House nearby. Guest lounge, beverage trays, TV in all rooms. Children welcome special rates. Leave M4 junction 28, take A48 towards Newport, at roundabout take third exit B4239 to St Brides, in village centre turn right (Church Rd), then left. Entrance off inn car park.

P ♞	SINGLE PER PERSON B&B		DOUBLE FOR 2 PERSONS B&B		🛏 3 🛏 3
🍴	MIN £	MAX £	MIN £	MAX £	OPEN
	20.00	25.00	36.00	38.00	1-12

GH	Wye View Holiday Apartments

HIGHLY COMMENDED

Riverside,
Guys Cliffe,
Tintern, Nr Chepstow
NP6 6SE
Tel: (01291) 689779

Wye View offers quality accommodation with three en-suite rooms all overlooking beautiful River Wye at Tintern on the A466 Chepstow/Monmouth road. Colour TV, tea/coffee making facilities in all rooms and a generous hearty breakfast. Gardens leading onto woodlands and only five minutes walk to Tintern Abbey, village inns and shops. A paradise for walkers, cyclists, fishermen, birdwatchers and tourists.

P ♞	SINGLE PER PERSON B&B		DOUBLE FOR 2 PERSONS B&B		🛏 3 🛏 3
	MIN £	MAX £	MIN £	MAX £	OPEN
	25.00	–	44.00	50.00	1-12

Welcome Host

Customer care is our top priority.

It's what our Welcome Host scheme is all about. Welcome Host badge and certificate holders are part of a tradition of friendliness. The Welcome Host programme, which is open to everyone from hotel staff to taxi drivers, places the emphasis on warm Welsh hospitality and first-class service.

GH	The Old Rectory

HIGHLY COMMENDED

Tintern,
Nr Chepstow
NP6 6SG
Tel: (01291) 689519
Fax: (0374) 570395

19th century old rectory in village of Tintern overlooking beautiful River Wye. Stunning views, log fires in winter. Four comfortably furnished bedrooms, two with private bathrooms, families welcome. Good cooking. Vegetarians catered for. Situated on A466 Chepstow to Monmouth road. Ten minutes walk from Tintern Abbey close to village inns and shops. Brochure available.

P ♞	SINGLE PER PERSON B&B		DOUBLE FOR 2 PERSONS B&B		🛏 4 🛏 2
🍴	MIN £	MAX £	MIN £	MAX £	OPEN
	–	–	34.00	38.00	1-12

GH	Valley House

COMMENDED

Raglan Road,
Tintern
NP6 6TH
Tel: (01291) 689652
Fax: (01291) 689805

18th century detached house in picturesque valley, 800 metres off A466, within one mile of Tintern Abbey. Beautiful en-suite rooms with colour TV, tea/coffee facilities and telephones. Freshly cooked hearty breakfasts served in our unique dining room with arched stone ceiling. Ideal base for touring Wye Valley, forest walks and numerous places to eat nearby.

P ♞	SINGLE PER PERSON B&B		DOUBLE FOR 2 PERSONS B&B		🛏 3 🛏
	MIN £	MAX £	MIN £	MAX £	OPEN
	–	–	38.00	40.00	1-12

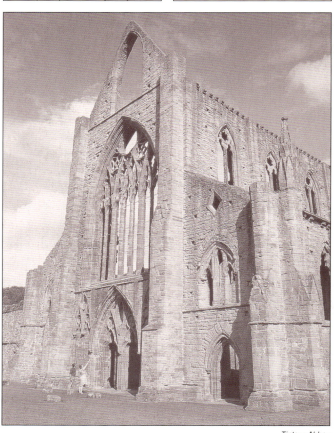

Tintern Abbey

Porthmadog Harbour

An Eventful Year

Here, we've listed just some of the events on offer, beginning with the main activities. More details of 1998 events are contained in a series of quarterly events leaflets available free from:

Wales Tourist Board, Davis Street, Cardiff CF1 2FU

Major Events

• End of May–end of December

Mid Wales Festival of the Countryside

A festival which brings together over 500 events taking place throughout beautiful Mid Wales – birdwatching, guided walks, arts and crafts, sheepdog trials, farm and garden visits. David Bellamy, a keen supporter, has called it 'the role model for sustainable tourism'.
Tel (01686) 625384

• 22–31 May

Hay Festival of Literature

Hay-on-Wye, the borderland 'town of books', provides an ideal setting for this literary festival with an international reputation. Attracts leading writers, poets and celebrities.
Tel (01497) 821217

• 7–12 July

Llangollen International Musical Eisteddfod

A colourful, cosmopolitan gathering of singers and dancers from all over the world perform in the beautiful little town of Llangollen. A unique festival first held in 1947 to help heal the wounds of war by bringing the peoples of the world together.
Tel (01978) 860236

• 20–23 July

Royal Welsh Show

Four days of fascination and entertainment at a show that attracts a wide audience to Builth Wells, not just from the farming community but from all walks of life. One of Wales's premier events, held in the heart of the country, covering all aspects of agriculture – and a lot more besides.
Tel (01982) 553683

• 1–8 August

Royal National Eisteddfod

Wales's most important cultural gathering, dating back to 1176, and held at a different venue each year. A festival dedicated to Welsh, Britain's oldest living language, with competitions, choirs, concerts, stands and exhibitions. Translation facilities available. This year's event will be held at Bridgend.
Tel (01222) 763777

• 7–9 August

Brecon Jazz

The streets of Brecon come alive with the sounds of summer jazz. A great three-day international festival with a wonderful atmosphere, which attracts the top names from the world of jazz. 'The most enjoyable of all Britain's festivals,' according to *The Times*.
Tel (01874) 625557

• 22–30 August

Llandrindod Wells Victorian Festival

The Mid Wales spa town of Llandrindod Wells celebrates its Victorian past. The festival includes street theatre, walks, talks, drama, exhibitions and music – all with a Victorian flavour.
Tel (01597) 823441

• 1 March–31 December

'50 Years at St Fagans', Museum of Welsh Life, near Cardiff

This open-air museum, one of the oldest in Europe, celebrates its 50th birthday in 1998 with a calendar of festivities, traditional and newly minted, which will reflect a kaleidoscope of Welsh history and culture spanning 400 years.

Within the museum's splendid parklands and grounds you can find farmhouses, a chapel, Victorian school, baker's shop, toll house, post office and craft workshops. These buildings are no pale imitation – they are the real thing, brought from all over Wales, reconstructed stone-by-stone, timber-by-timber, and peopled by skilled craftsmen who recreate the daily life of rural Wales.

During the 50th birthday year, these historic buildings will form the backdrop for all kinds of special events:

Gŵyl Ifan Folk Festival

Everyman Theatre Festival

1 March	Celebration of St David's Day and launch of 50th anniversary
18-19 April	Historic Car Rally
25-26 April	Forest Fair – competitions and demonstrations showing the importance of forestry skills in the history of Wales
2-4 May	May Fair and Battle of St Fagans, a spectacular re-enactment of an important Civil War battle of 1648 by thousands of members of the Sealed Knot
6 June	Miners' Gala (processions, bands, choirs and banners) and Paul Robeson Centenary Concert
13 June	Gŵyl y Plant – colourful Festival of Children's Folk Dancing
20-21 June	Gŵyl Ifan – Annual Folk Dancing Spectacular, combined this year with a Welsh Folk Festival
21 June	Cymanfa Ganu – Festival of Welsh Hymn-Singing
4 July	Happy Birthday Museum of Welsh Life – a day-long celebration based around the reopening of the elegant St Fagans Castle following refurbishment. Entry at 1948 prices! Evening events (separate charge) include music from 50 years and fireworks
22 July-1 August	Everyman Theatre Festival, with open-air Shakespeare in woodland setting
29-31 August	Youthful Promise Wales – operatic concerts featuring aspiring young Welsh singers, the stars of tomorrow
26-27 September	Gŵyl Fihangel – Harvest Festival celebrating 400 years of Welsh food and farming customs
31 October	Calan Gaeaf – Halloween Event with torchlit ghost tours and seasonal suppers
2-5 December	Festive Christmas Tree events, bringing to life Christmas customs past and present

For further information please contact the Museum of Welsh Life, St Fagans, Cardiff CF5 6XB. Tel (01222) 573500

Events for Everyone

late 1997-28 February
Welsh National Opera Spring Season in Cardiff, New Theatre

7 February
Wales v Italy Rugby International, Cardiff RFC Ground, Cardiff Arms Park

1 March
St David's Day Concert, St David's Hall, Cardiff

6-8 March
Folk Weekend, Llanwrtyd Wells

26 March
Conwy Seed Fair

14-18 April
Welsh National Opera Spring Season in Swansea, Grand Theatre

24 April
BBC National Orchestra of Wales 70th Birthday Concert, St David's Hall, Cardiff

4-9 May
Llandrindod Wells Drama Festival

8-10 May
Llangollen International Jazz Festival

14-17 May
Llantilio Crossenny Festival of Music and Drama, nr Abergavenny

23-25 May
Hay Children's Festival of the Arts, Hay-on-Wye

23-31 May
St David's Cathedral Festival

24-25 May
Crafts in Action, St Donat's Castle, nr Llantwit Major

25 May
Fete & Gala, Merthyr Tydfil

25-30 May
Urdd National Eisteddfod (Youth Eisteddfod), Pwllheli

6 June
4th Llangollen Choral Festival

13 June
Man v Horse Marathon, Llanwrtyd Wells

16-21 June
Criccieth Festival

19-21 June
Gŵyl Ifan – Welsh Folk Dancing Festival, Cardiff and district

Welsh Open Golf Stroke Play Championship, Southerndown Golf Club, nr Bridgend

20-25 June
Barmouth to Fort William Three Peaks Yacht Race

25-28 June
Gŵyl Gregynog Festival, nr Newtown

3-5 July
Beyond the Border – Welsh International Festival of Storytelling, St Donat's Castle, nr Llantwit Major

Morris in the Forest (Morris dancing, forest walks, etc), Llanwrtyd Wells

North Wales Bluegrass Music Festival, Conwy

11-12 July
Mid Wales Festival of Transport, Powis Castle, Welshpool

14-18 July
Saundersfoot in Bloom Flower Festival

17-25 July
Welsh Proms, St David's Hall, Cardiff

20-25 July
Ian Rush International Soccer Tournament, Aberystwyth

20 July-1 August
Gower Music Festival

25 July-1 August
Fishguard Music Festival

27 July-1 August
Welsh Amateur Golf Championship, Prestatyn Golf Club

1 August
Brecon County Show

1-8 August
Llanwrtyd Wells Festival Week

4-8 August
Girls' British Open Amateur Golf Championship, Holyhead Golf Club

6-9 August
Mountain Bike Festival, Llanwrtyd Wells

8 August
Chepstow Agricultural Show

13-14 August
United Counties Show, Carmarthen

14-16 August
Cardigan Bay Regatta, New Quay Harbour

19 August
Vale of Glamorgan Agricultural Show, Fonmon Castle Park, nr Barry

22 August
Talybont and North Cardiganshire Agricultural and Horticultural Show, Talybont, nr Borth

24 August
World Bog-Snorkelling Championships, Llanwrtyd Wells

26 August
Llangeitho Agricultural and Horticultural Show, nr Tregaron

27 August
Monmouthshire Show, Monmouth

27 August-1 September
Presteigne Festival of Music and the Arts

31 August
Merthyr Show, Merthyr Tydfil

4-12 September
Barmouth Arts Festival

5 September
Llandysul and District Agricultural Show

9-11 September
Home International Golf Championship, Royal Porthcawl Golf Club

12 September
Usk Show

14 September
Conwy Honey Fair

15-18 September
Welsh International Four Days Walks, Llanwrtyd Wells

1-31 October
Tydfil Festival, Merthyr Tydfil

3-24 October
Swansea Festival of Music and the Arts

10-11 October
49th South Wales Miners' Eisteddfod, Grand Pavilion, Porthcawl

15-18 October
Welsh International Four Days Cycle Rides, Llanwrtyd Wells

20 October
Welsh Dairy Show, United Counties Showground, Carmarthen

13-22 November
Mid Wales Beer Festival, Llanwrtyd Wells

Welsh International Film Festival, Aberystwyth

8 December
Royal Welsh Agricultural Winter Fair, Builth Wells

Gwyliau Cymru/ Festivals of Wales

This is the collective voice for around 50 arts festivals held the length and breadth of Wales, embracing everything from classical music to jazz, children's events to drama.
For more information, please contact:

**Festivals of Wales,
PO Box 62, Newtown SY16 3WD
Tel (01686) 640766**

Makers of Wales, the Millennium Festival Campaign for Wales, is all about the people of Wales and how, over time, they have created a unique identity through the country's language and customs, together with its built and natural heritage. The festival theme for 1998 is 'Transport and Communications'. Throughout the year there will be events and exhibitions staged by many organisations ranging from local community groups to Cadw-Welsh Historic Monuments, the Countryside Council for Wales, the National Museums and Galleries of Wales and the National Trust. Look out for the distinctive Makers of Wales symbol on your travels.

**Further details from: Campaign Co-ordinator,
Makers of Wales, 4th Floor, Empire House, Cardiff CF1 6DN
Tel (01222) 471121**

BEACHES GUIDE

On these pages, we introduce you to some of the best of our many beautiful Welsh beaches. Our choice is based on beaches which have been awarded the coveted European Blue Flag or Tidy Britain Group Seaside Award. All beaches featured satisfy EC Standards of water quality, so you can enjoy them safe in the knowledge that the water is as appealing as the surroundings.

European Blue Flag

Nine beaches in Wales were awarded this prestigious flag in 1997 – Aberystwyth North, Barmouth, Cefn Sidan (Pembrey), Llanddwyn (Newborough), Port Eynon, Pwllheli, Tenby North, Tywyn and Whitesand Bay (St David's).

The Blue Flag, Europe's highest accolade for beaches, is awarded annually. It is based on a total of 26 criteria covering such items as bathing water quality and safety, beach cleanliness, services, wheelchair access, dog control, first aid and so on. Blue Flag beaches must satisfy EC Guideline water quality standards, which are 20 times more stringent than EC Mandatory standards.

Tidy Britain Group Seaside Award

Seaside Award beaches fly a distinctive blue and yellow flag representing sea and sand. The award identifies well-managed beaches where you can be assured of excellent standards of cleanliness and safety, together with water quality which complies with current European legislation (the EC Mandatory standard). There are two categories of award beach – Resort and Rural.

A **Seaside Award Resort** beach actively encourages visitors, provides facilities and offers a variety of activities. Award-winning beaches are usually found near a town with access by public transport, and you can normally expect to find a café or restaurant, toilets and public telephones at the beach. Dogs have restricted access. Each beach fulfils 29 criteria, falling into five groups – safety, management, cleanliness, information and water quality.

A **Seaside Award Rural** beach has few facilities. It is usually more remote than a resort beach so is enjoyed more for its natural environment. Award-winning rural beaches fulfil 13 criteria falling into the same five groups as resort beaches, but are not expected to provide the same facilities. Dogs may be allowed on rural beaches.

Green Sea

This ambitious coastal environmental scheme was launched in 1996. Green Sea is a unique initiative which aims to harness the 'power of partnership' to create real improvements in the quality of the seas and coastline of Wales. A key goal for the initiative is the achievement of the coveted European Blue Flag Award for 50 Welsh beaches: since its launch, the number of Blue Flag beaches in Wales has increased from four in 1996 to today's nine. Green Sea's long-term goal is for Wales to have the best managed beaches in the UK and Europe.

Green Sea is supported by an informal group of over 40 Welsh organisations from the public, private and voluntary sectors with an interest in the coastal environment.

ALL ALONG
the Coast

Whitesand Bay, St David's

Key

● European Blue Flag Award beach 1997. Water quality must be at least EC Guideline standard (excellent)

● Seaside Award Resort beach 1997. Water quality must be at least EC Mandatory standard (good)

● Seaside Award Rural beach 1997. Water quality must be at least EC Mandatory standard (good)

All featured beaches were monitored during the 1996 bathing season between May and September and met standards equivalent to those used by the UK Government for compliance with the EC Directive Mandatory (I) standard for water quality. The list was compiled with the assistance of Dŵr Cymru/Welsh Water, the Environment Agency, Hyder Laboratories and all coastal local authorities in Wales.

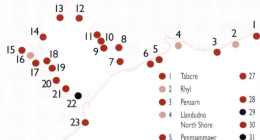
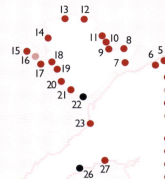

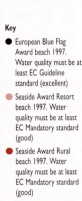
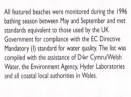

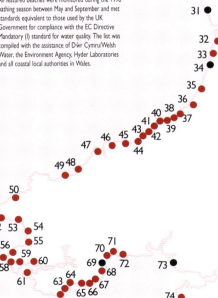
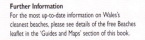

1	Talacre	27	Criccieth East (West End)	53	Newgale
2	Rhyl	28	Llandanwg	54	Nolton Haven
3	Pensarn	29	Barmouth	55	Broad Haven
4	Llandudno North Shore	30	Fairbourne	56	St Bride's Haven
5	Penmaenmawr	31	Tywyn	57	Martin's Haven
6	Llanfairfechan	32	Borth	58	Marloes
7	Beaumaris	33	Clarach	59	Dale
8	Llanddona	34	Aberystwyth North, Traeth y Gogledd	60	Gelliswick, nr Milford Haven
9	Benllech	35	Llanrhystyd	61	West Angle Bay
10	Moelfre	36	Aberaeron, Traeth y De/ South Beach	62	Broad Haven South
11	Traeth Lligwy, Moelfre	37	New Quay, Traeth Gwyn	63	Barafundle Bay
12	Porth Eilian, Llaneilian	38	New Quay Harbour	64	Freshwater East
13	Cemaes Bay	39	New Quay, Traeth y Dolau	65	Manorbier
14	Porth Tywyn Mawr, Sandy Beach	40	Cwm Tudu	66	Skrinkle, nr Lydstep
15	Porth Dafarch, nr Trearddur Bay	41	Cil Borth, nr Llangrannog	67	Lydstep
16	Trearddur Bay	42	Llangrannog	68	Tenby South
17	Borth Wen, Rhoscolyn	43	Penbryn	69	Tenby North
18	Traeth Llydan, Silver Bay	44	Tre-saith	70	Coppet Hall, nr Saundersfoot
19	Rhosneigr	45	Aberporth West, Traeth y Dolwen	71	Wiseman's Bridge, nr Saundersfoot
20	Porth Nobla, Llanfaelog	46	Mwnt	72	Amroth
21	Traeth Mawr, Aberffraw	47	Poppit Sands West	73	Cefn Sidan, Pembrey
22	Llanddwyn, Newborough	48	Newport North	74	Rhossili/ Llangennith
23	Dinas Dinlle	49	Cwm-yr-Eglwys	75	Port Eynon
24	Aberdaron	50	Aber Eiddi	76	Oxwich Bay
25	Abersoch	51	Whitesand Bay, St David's	77	Caswell Bay
26	Pwllheli, Marian y De	52	Caerfai, St David's	78	Porthcawl Rest Bay
				79	Southerndown

Further Information
For the most up-to-date information on Wales's cleanest beaches, please see details of the free Beaches leaflet in the 'Guides and Maps' section of this book.

SO
Accessible

One of Wales's big advantages is its ease of access. It's only a few hours by road and rail from most of the UK's main centres. Travel to Wales doesn't take up much time or money, so you can enjoy your holiday or short break to the full. And when you arrive, you'll be back in the days when driving was a pleasure on traffic-free highways and byways.

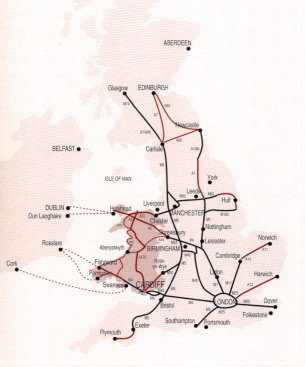

MILEAGE CHART

	miles	journey time by car
Birmingham–Aberystwyth	125	2hrs 50mins
Canterbury–Cardiff	219	4hrs
Coventry–Barmouth	133	2hrs 50mins
Exeter–Swansea	161	2hrs 20mins
Leeds–Llandudno	131	2hrs
London–Cardiff	155	2hrs 40mins
London–Tenby	245	4hrs 10mins
Manchester–Caernarfon	110	2hrs
Nottingham–Swansea	202	3hrs 10mins
Peterborough–Aberystwyth	208	4hrs 30mins
Newcastle-upon-Tyne–Llandudno	230	4hrs
Reading–Carmarthen	177	2hrs 40mins
York–Welshpool	155	3hrs

By Car

Travel to South and West Wales is easy on the M4 and onward dual carriageway systems. With the opening of the Second Severn Crossing, traffic for Cardiff and West Wales follows the revised route of the M4 across the new bridge. For Chepstow and the Wye Valley you'll need the M48 (the old route of the M4) across the original bridge. In North Wales, the A55 coastal 'Expressway' whisks traffic past the old bottlenecks, including Conwy. Mid Wales is easily reached by the M54 which links with the M6/M5/M1.

Driving around Wales is a delight, for most highways remain blissfully quiet and uncrowded apart from a few peak summer weekends. Wales is a small yet scenically varied country, so there's no need to rush – take your time and enjoy it to the full.

By Train

Fast and frequent Great Western InterCity services run between London Paddington and Cardiff (via Reading and Swindon), taking only two hours. This hourly service (every half hour at peak times) also runs to Newport, Bridgend, Port Talbot, Neath and Swansea, with onward connections to West Wales. Fast Virgin West Coast trains link London Euston with the North Wales coast, serving both Bangor and Holyhead, and Virgin CrossCountry runs a service between the North East of England and South Wales.

In addition, Wales and West Passenger Train Company runs Alphaline services direct from London Waterloo (via Woking and Basingstoke) to Cardiff and other main stations in South and West Wales and the Welsh Marches. There are also convenient and comfortable Alphaline trains direct to Cardiff (some running through to South-West Wales) from:

• Manchester/the North West

• Brighton/Portsmouth/Salisbury/Southampton

• The West of England/Bristol

• Nottingham/Birmingham/Gloucester

For Mid Wales there are Alphaline trains to Aberystwyth and other Mid Wales resorts from Birmingham via Shrewsbury. This service connects with Virgin trains from London Euston at Birmingham.

North West Express train services run direct from Manchester and Birmingham to most resorts on the North Wales coast via Chester.

Exploring Wales by train is a delight. Scenic routes include the beautiful Heart of Wales line from Shrewsbury to Swansea via Llanelli, the Conwy Valley line from Llandudno Junction to Blaenau Ffestiniog, and the Cambrian Coast line, which runs along the mountain-backed shoreline from Pwllheli to Machynlleth and Aberystwyth.

Ask about the money-saving unlimited-travel Rover and Flexi Pass fares, some of which include the use of bus services.

Train information

For all enquiries please telephone (0345) 484950, or contact your local travel agent or principal station. Rail Rover and Flexi Pass details and tickets are also available from (01766) 512340.

By Coach

National Express provides a nationwide network of express coach services, many of which have been upgraded to Rapide specification with on-board washrooms and light refreshments available. Convenient services to Wales operate from London's Victoria Coach Station and from almost all other major towns and cities in England and Scotland.

Towns and resorts throughout Wales are, of course, connected by a whole range of local and regional services. Details from Tourist Information Centres and local bus stations. You can travel cross-country by the TrawsCambria service running between Cardiff and Bangor (via Aberystwyth). Within North and Mid Wales you can combine local bus and train services through unlimited-travel Rover tickets (see 'By Train' for details).

Coach information

Contact your local travel agent or National Express office. For further information and all National Express credit/debit card bookings please telephone (0990) 808080. For details of your nearest National Express agent please telephone (0990) 010104 (calls cost a maximum of 8p per minute, less at off-peak times).

National Travel Hotline – (0891) 910910

One call covers it all. Phone this number for information on all of Britain's train, express coach and rural bus services – and you can also make credit card bookings at the same time. The hotline is open 6am–9pm seven days a week (calls cost 50p per minute).

By Sea

Five services operate across the Irish Sea:

- Cork to Swansea
  (Swansea-Cork Ferries,
  tel 01792-456116)

- Dublin to Holyhead
  (Irish Ferries, tel 0990-171717 General Enquiries, 0345-171717 Firm Bookings)

- Dun Laoghaire to Holyhead
  (Stena Line High-Speed Superferry, tel 0990-707070)

- Rosslare to Fishguard
  (Stena Line – a choice of two services: Sea Lynx Catamaran and Superferry, tel 0990-707070)

- Rosslare to Pembroke
  (Irish Ferries, tel 0990-171717 General Enquiries, 0345-171717 Firm Bookings)

By Air

There are direct flights from Aberdeen, Amsterdam, Belfast, Brussels, Channel Islands, Dublin, Edinburgh, Glasgow, Isle of Man, Manchester and Paris to Cardiff International Airport (tel 01446-711111), 12 miles from the city centre. There are many worldwide connections to Cardiff via most of these airports. A rail/air link coach service runs from the airport to Cardiff's central train and bus stations.

Manchester and Birmingham Airports are also convenient gateways for Wales.

Wales's Narrow-Gauge Railways

There are eight members of Wales's narrow-gauge 'Great Little Trains': Bala Lake Railway, Brecon Mountain Railway (Merthyr Tydfil), Ffestiniog Railway (Porthmadog), Llanberis Lake Railway, Talyllyn Railway (Tywyn), Vale of Rheidol Railway (Aberystwyth), Welsh Highland Railway (Porthmadog) and Welshpool and Llanfair Railway (Llanfair Caereinion). Details are available from The Great Little Trains of Wales, FREEPOST, The Station, Llanfair Caereinion SY21 0BR (tel 01938-810441).

The railways operating independently of 'Great Little Trains' are: Fairbourne and Barmouth Steam Railway (tel 01341-250362), Gwili Railway, near Carmarthen (tel 01267-230666), Llangollen Railway (tel 01978-860951), Snowdon Mountain Railway, Llanberis (tel 01286-870223), Teifi Valley Railway, near Newcastle Emlyn (tel 01559-371077) and Welsh Highland Railway/Rheilffordd Eryri (the new northern leg of the line operating from Caernarfon, scheduled to open Easter 1998 – tel 01766-512340).

Make the most of your stay in Wales by contacting one of our Tourist Information Centres for help on all aspects of your holiday. TIC staff will be delighted to assist with • booking your accommodation (see below) • places to visit • places to eat • things to do • routes to take • national and local events • maps, guides and books

Tourist Information Centres

Normal opening times are 10am–5.30pm. These hours may vary to suit local circumstances. Those marked with an asterisk (*) are open seasonally only (April–September). TICs operate a Bed Booking Service which covers local accommodation together with places throughout Wales and the UK. A small charge may be made for this service.

Accommodating Wheelchair Users TICs are assessed for access by wheelchair users, based on the following criteria:
Grade 1 Accessible to a wheelchair user travelling independently **Grade 2** Accessible to a wheelchair user travelling with assistance
Grade 3 Accessible to a wheelchair user able to walk a few paces and up to a maximum of three steps • Awaiting Grading

			Access Grade
Aberaeron	The Quay, Aberaeron SA46 0BT	Tel (01545) 570602	2
Aberdyfi/Aberdovey *	Wharf Gardens, Aberdyfi LL35 0ED	Tel (01654) 767321	2
Abergavenny	Swan Meadow, Monmouth Road, Abergavenny NP7 5HH	Tel (01873) 857588	1
Aberystwyth	Terrace Road, Aberystwyth SY23 2AG	Tel (01970) 612125	2
Bala	Penllyn, Pensarn Road, Bala LL23 7SR	Tel (01678) 521021	1
Bangor *	Town Hall, Deiniol Road, Bangor LL57 2RE	Tel (01248) 352786	2
Barmouth *	Old Library, Station Road, Barmouth LL42 1LU	Tel (01341) 280787	2
Barry Island *	The Triangle, Paget Road, Barry Island CF62 5TQ	Tel (01446) 747171	2
Betws-y-Coed	Royal Oak Stables, Betws-y-Coed LL24 0AH	Tel (01690) 710426	2
Blaenau Ffestiniog *	Isallt, High Street, Blaenau Ffestiniog LL41 3HD	Tel (01766) 830360	2
Borth *	Cambrian Terrace, Borth SY24 5HU	Tel (01970) 871174	2
Brecon	Cattle Market Car Park, Brecon LD3 9DA	Tel (01874) 622485	2
Broad Haven *	National Park Car Park, Broad Haven SA62 3JH	Tel (01437) 781412	2
Builth Wells *	Groe Car Park, Builth Wells LD2 3BT	Tel (01982) 553307	2
Caerleon *	5 High Street, Caerleon NP6 1AE	Tel (01633) 422656	2
Caernarfon	Oriel Pendeitsh, Castle Street, Caernarfon LL55 2NA	Tel (01286) 672232	2
Caerphilly	Lower Twyn Square, Caerphilly CF83 1XX	Tel (01222) 880011	1
Cardiff	Central Station, Cardiff CF1 1QY	Tel (01222) 227281	2
Cardigan	Theatr Mwldan, Bath House Road, Cardigan SA43 2JY	Tel (01239) 613230	2
Carmarthen	Lammas Street, Carmarthen SA31 3AQ	Tel (01267) 231557	2
Chepstow	Castle Car Park, Bridge Street, Chepstow NP6 5EY	Tel (01291) 623772	1
Colwyn Bay	40 Station Road, Colwyn Bay LL29 8BU	Tel (01492) 530478	2
Conwy	Conwy Castle Visitor Centre, Conwy LL32 8LD	Tel (01492) 592248	2
Corris *	Craft Centre, Corris, nr Machynlleth SY20 9SP	Tel (01654) 761244	2
Crickhowell *	Beaufort Chambers, Beaufort Street, Crickhowell NP8 1AA	Tel (01873) 812105	2
Cwmcarn *	Cwmcarn Forest Drive Centre, Nantcarn Road, Cwmcarn, nr Cross Keys NP2 7FA	Tel (01495) 272001	2
Dolgellau	Tŷ Meirion, Eldon Square, Dolgellau LL40 1PU	Tel (01341) 422888	2
Elan Valley *	Elan Valley Visitor Centre, Elan Valley, nr Rhayader LD6 5HP	Tel (01597) 810898	2
Ewloe *	Gateway Services, A55 Westbound, Northophall, Ewloe CH7 6HE	Tel (01244) 541597	3
Fishguard Harbour *	Passenger Concourse, The Harbour, Goodwick, Fishguard SA64 0BU	Tel (01348) 872037	2
Fishguard Town	4 Hamilton Street, Fishguard SA64 9HL	Tel (01348) 873484	2
Harlech *	Gwyddfor House, High Street, Harlech LL46 2YA	Tel (01766) 780658	2
Haverfordwest	Old Bridge, Haverfordwest SA61 2EZ	Tel (01437) 763110	1
Holyhead	The Kiosk, Stena Line, Terminal 1, Holyhead LL65 1DR	Tel (01407) 762622	2
Kilgetty	Kingsmoor Common, Kilgetty SA68 0YA	Tel (01834) 814161	•
Knighton	Offa's Dyke Centre, West Street, Knighton LD7 1EW	Tel (01547) 528753	3
Lake Vyrnwy *	Unit 2, Vyrnwy Craft Workshops, Lake Vyrnwy SY10 0LY	Tel (01691) 870346	2
Llanberis	41a High Street, Llanberis LL55 4EU	Tel (01286) 870765	1
Llandarcy	BP Club, Llandarcy, Neath SA10 6HJ	Tel (01792) 813030	2
Llandeilo *	Car Park, Crescent Road, Llandeilo SA19 6HN	Tel (01558) 824226	3

Llandovery	King's Road, Llandovery SA20 0AW	Tel (01550) 720693	2
Llandrindod Wells	Old Town Hall, Memorial Gardens, Llandrindod Wells LD1 5DL	Tel (01597) 822600	2
Llandudno	1–2 Chapel Street, Llandudno LL30 2YU	Tel (01492) 876413	2
Llanelli	Public Library, Vaughan Street, Llanelli SA15 3AS	Tel (01554) 772020	2
Llanfairpwllgwyngyll	Station Site, Llanfairpwllgwyngyll LL61 5UJ	Tel (01248) 713177	1
Llangollen	Town Hall, Castle Street, Llangollen LL20 5PD	Tel (01978) 860828	2
Llanidloes	Town Hall, Great Oak Street, Llanidloes SY18 6BN	Tel (01686) 412605	2
Llanwrtyd Wells *	Tŷ Barcud, The Square, Llanwrtyd Wells LD5 4RB	Tel (01591) 610666	2
Machynlleth	Canolfan Owain Glyndŵr, Machynlleth SY20 8EE	Tel (01654) 702401	2
Magor	First Services and Lodge, Junction 23a M4, Magor NP6 3YL	Tel (01633) 881122	1
Merthyr Tydfil	14a Glebeland Street, Merthyr Tydfil CF47 8AU	Tel (01685) 379884	1
Milford Haven *	94 Charles Street, Milford Haven SA73 2HL	Tel (01646) 690866	2
Mold *	Library, Museum and Art Gallery, Earl Road, Mold CH7 1AP	Tel (01352) 759331	1
Monmouth *	Shire Hall, Agincourt Square, Monmouth NP5 3DY	Tel (01600) 713899	2
Mumbles *	Oystermouth Square, Mumbles, Swansea SA3 4DQ	Tel (01792) 361302	3
New Quay *	Church Street, New Quay SA45 9NZ	Tel (01545) 560865	1
Newcastle Emlyn *	Market Hall, Newcastle Emlyn SA38 9AE	Tel (01239) 711333	2
Newport	Museum and Art Gallery, John Frost Square, Newport NP9 1HZ	Tel (01633) 842962	1
Newport (Pembrokeshire) *	2 Bank Cottages, Long Street, Newport SA42 0TL	Tel (01239) 820912	3
Newtown	The Park, Back Lane, Newtown SY16 2PW	Tel (01686) 625580	●
Pembroke *	Visitor Centre, Commons Road, Pembroke SA71 4EA	Tel (01646) 622388	2
Pembroke Dock *	The Guntower, Front Street SA72 6JZ	Tel (01646) 622246	1
Penarth *	Penarth Pier, The Esplanade, Penarth CF64 3AU	Tel (01222) 708849	3
Pont Abraham	Pont Abraham Services, Junction 49 M4, Llanedi SA4 1FP	Tel (01792) 883838	2
Pontneddfechan *	nr Glyn Neath SA11 5NR	Tel (01639) 721795	1
Pontypridd	Historical Centre, The Old Bridge, Pontypridd CF37 3PE	Tel (01443) 409512	2
Porthcawl *	Old Police Station, John Street, Porthcawl CF36 3DT	Tel (01656) 786639	2
Porthmadog	High Street, Porthmadog LL49 9LP	Tel (01766) 512981	2
Prestatyn *	Offa's Dyke Centre, Central Beach, Prestatyn LL19 7EY	Tel (01745) 889092	●
Presteigne *	Shire Hall, Presteigne LD8 2AD	Tel (01544) 260650	2
Pwllheli	Min y Don, Station Square, Pwllheli LL53 5HG	Tel (01758) 613000	2
Rhayader *	Leisure Centre, Rhayader LD6 5BU	Tel (01597) 810591	2
Rhos on Sea *	The Promenade, Rhos on Sea LL28 4EP	Tel (01492) 548778	1
Rhyl	Rhyl Children's Village, West Parade, Rhyl LL18 1HZ	Tel (01745) 355068	2
Ruthin	Ruthin Craft Centre, Park Road, Ruthin LL15 1BB	Tel (01824) 703992	2
St David's	City Hall, St David's SA62 6SD	Tel (01437) 720392	2
Sarn	Sarn Park Services, Junction 36 M4, nr Bridgend CF32 9SY	Tel (01656) 654906	1
Saundersfoot *	The Barbecue, Harbour Car Park, Saundersfoot SA69 9HE	Tel (01834) 813672	2
Swansea	PO Box 59, Singleton Street, Swansea SA1 3QG	Tel (01792) 468321	1
Tenby	The Croft, Tenby SA70 8AP	Tel (01834) 842402	1
Tywyn *	High Street, Tywyn LL36 9AD	Tel (01654) 710070	2
Welshpool	Vicarage Garden, Church Street, Welshpool SY21 7DD	Tel (01938) 552043	1
Wrexham	Lambpit Street, Wrexham LL11 1WN	Tel (01978) 292015	2
And at Oswestry on the Wales/England border			
Heritage Centre,	2 Church Terrace, Oswestry SY11 2TE	Tel (01691) 662753	3
Mile End Services,	Oswestry SY11 4JA	Tel (01691) 662488	1

Wales in London's West End

If you're in London, call in at the Wales Information Bureau for everything you need to plan your visit to Wales. Until March, the Bureau is located at the British Travel Centre, 12 Lower Regent Street, Piccadilly Circus, London SW1Y 4PQ. Tel (0171) 409 0969. After March, the Bureau moves to the British Travel Centre, 1 Regent Street, London SW1Y 4NS.

FURTHER
Information

The following organisations and authorities will be pleased to provide any further information you require when planning your holiday to Wales.

Wales Tourist Board

Dept BB2
Davis Street
Cardiff CF1 2FU
Tel (01222) 475226

WALES ON THE
WEB

Make the most of your visit to Wales by calling into the **NEW** Wales Tourist Board site from mid-January 1998. It's your easy route to up-to-date information on accommodation, attractions and events in Wales, as well as ideas for itineraries and themes to explore. Just dial into 'Wales on the Web' at:

www.tourism.wales.gov.uk

Holiday information is also available from:

North Wales Tourism

Dept BB2
77 Conway Road
Colwyn Bay LL29 7BL
Tel (01492) 531731

Mid Wales Tourism

Dept BB2
The Station
Machynlleth SY20 8TG
Tel (01654) 702653

Tourism South and West Wales

Dept BB2
Charter Court
Enterprise Park
Swansea SA7 9DB
Tel (01792) 781212

Tourism South and West Wales

Dept BB2
Old Bridge
Haverfordwest SA61 2EZ
Tel (01437) 766388
(quote Dept BB2)

Other Useful Addresses

Brecon Beacons National Park

7 Glamorgan Street
Brecon LD3 7DP
Tel (01874) 624437

Cadw: Welsh Historic Monuments

Crown Building
Cathays Park
Cardiff CF1 3NQ
Tel (01222) 500200

Environment Agency

(Fisheries and Conservation enquiries)
Plas-yr-Afon
St Mellons Business Park
St Mellons
Cardiff CF3 0LT
Tel (01222) 770088

Football Association of Wales

3 Westgate Street
Cardiff CF1 1DD
Tel (01222) 372325

Forestry Enterprise (Forestry Commission)

Victoria House
Victoria Terrace
Aberystwyth SY23 2DQ
Tel (01970) 612367

National Trust

North Wales Regional Office
Trinity Square
Llandudno LL30 2DE
Tel (01492) 860123

National Trust

South Wales Regional Office
The King's Head
Bridge Street
Llandeilo SA19 6BB
Tel (01558) 822800

Offa's Dyke Association

West Street
Knighton LD7 1EN
Tel (01547) 528753

Pembrokeshire Coast National Park

Wynch Lane
Haverfordwest SA61 1PY
Tel (01437) 764636

Ramblers' Association in Wales

Ty'r Cerddwyr
High Street
Gresford
Wrexham LL12 8PT
Tel (01978) 855148

Snowdonia National Park Authority

Penrhyndeudraeth LL48 6LF
Tel (01766) 770274

Surfcall Wales

(daily surf/weather conditions at all major beaches)

Tel (0839) 505697/360361
Calls cost 49p per minute

Taste of Wales- *Blas ar Gymru*

The Food Hall
Royal Welsh Showground
Llanelwedd
Builth Wells LD2 3SY
Tel (01982) 552952

Wales Craft Council

Park Lane House
7 High Street
Welshpool SY21 7JP
Tel (01938) 555313

Welsh Golfing Union

Catsash
Newport NP6 1JQ
Tel (01633) 430830

Welsh Rugby Union

Cardiff Arms Park
PO Box 22
Cardiff CF1 1JL
Tel (01222) 390111

Youth Hostels Association

1 Cathedral Road
Cardiff CF1 9HA
Tel (01222) 396766

Trespass – a word of warning

If you're out and about enjoying an activity holiday – walking off established footpaths, mountain biking, or even landing your paraglider – please obtain permission from the landowners. To avoid any problems, it's always best to seek out the appropriate permission beforehand.

Information for Visitors with Disabilities

Discovering Accessible Wales

is an information-packed guide for visitors who may have impaired movement or are confined to a wheelchair. The book is available free from the Wales Tourist Board. See 'Publications, Guides and Maps' section for details.

For details of other wheelchair-accessible accommodation inspected to the same standards please contact the Holiday Care Service. This organisation also provides a wide range of other travel and holiday information for disabled visitors:

Holiday Care Service

2nd Floor
Imperial Buildings
Victoria Road
Horley
Surrey RH6 7PZ
Tel (01293) 774535

Other Helpful Organisations

Disability Wales

Llys Ifor
Crescent Road
Caerphilly CF83 1XL
Tel (01222) 887325

Wales Council for the Blind

3rd Floor
Shand House
20 Newport Road
Cardiff CF2 1DB
Tel (01222) 473954

Wales Council for the Deaf

Glenview House
Courthouse Street
Pontypridd CF37 1JY
Tel (01443) 485687
Fax (01443) 408555
Minicom (01443) 485686

British Tourist Authority Overseas Offices

Your enquiries will be welcome at the offices of the British Tourist Authority in the following countries:

Argentina
BTA, Avenida Cordoba 645, 2nd Floor,
1054 Buenos Aires
(open to the public 1000-1300 only)
Tel (1) 314 6735   Fax (1) 314 8955

Australia
BTA, Level 16, Gateway, 1 Macquarie Place,
Sydney, NSW 2000
Tel (2) 9377 4400   Fax (2) 9377 4499

Belgium
BTA, 306 Avenue Louise, 1050 Brussels
Tel (2) 646 35 10   Fax (2) 646 39 86

Brazil
BTA, Avenida Nilo Pecanha 50/1103,
20044-900 Rio de Janeiro-RJ
Tel (21) 220 1187/7072   Fax (21) 240 8779

Canada
BTA, 111 Avenue Road, Suite 450, Toronto,
Ontario M5R 3J8
Tel (1) 416 925 6326   Fax (1) 416 961 2175

Czech and Slovak Republics
BTA, Kaprova 13, 110 01 Prague 1 *(visitors)*
PO Box 264, 110 01, Prague 01 *(mail)*
Tel (2) 232 7213/2520   Fax (2) 232 7469

Denmark
BTA, Møntergade 3, 1116 Copenhagen K
Tel 33 33 91 88   Fax 33 14 01 36

Finland
British Travel Centre, Mikonkatu 13A,
00100 Helsinki
Tel (0) 630 912   Fax (0) 622 1562

France
BTA, Maison de la Grande-Bretagne,
19 rue des Mathurins, 75009 Paris
Tel (1) 44 51 56 20   Fax (1) 44 51 56 21
Minitel 3615 BRITISH

Germany
BTA, Taunusstrasse 52-60, 60329 Frankfurt
Tel (69) 238 0711   Fax (69) 238 0717

Hong Kong
BTA, Room 1504, Eton Tower, 8 Hysan Avenue,
Causeway Bay, Hong Kong
Tel 2882 9967   Fax 2577 1443

Ireland
BTA, 18-19 College Green, Dublin 2
Tel (1) 670 8000   Fax (1) 670 8244

Italy (Milan)
BTA, Corso Magenta 32, 20123 Milano
Tel (2) 7201 0078   Fax (2) 7201 0086

Italy (Rome)
BTA, Corso Vittorio Emanuele 337,
00186 Rome
Tel (6) 688 06821   Fax (6) 687 9095

Japan (Osaka)
BTA, OCAT Building 4th Floor, 1-chome,
4-1 Minatomachi, Naniwa-ku, Osaka 556
Tel (6) 635 3093   Fax (6) 635 3095

Japan (Tokyo)
BTA, Akasaka Twin Tower 1F, 2-17-22 Akasaka,
Minato-ku, Tokyo
Tel (3) 5562 2550   Fax (3) 5562 2551

Korea
BTA, Anglican Church Building,
3-7 Chung-dong, Choong-ku, Seoul 100-120
Tel (2) 723 8266-8   Fax (2) 720 6066

Netherlands
BTA, Aurora Gebouw (5e), Stadhouderskade 2,
1054 ES Amsterdam
Tel (20) 685 5051   Fax (20) 618 6868

New Zealand
BTA, 3rd Floor, Dilworth Building, corner
Queen and Customs Streets, Auckland 1
Tel (9) 303 1446   Fax (9) 377 6965

Norway
BTA, Nedre Slotts Gt 21, 4 etasje,
N-0157 Oslo *(visitors)*
Postbox 1554 Vika, N-0117 Oslo *(mail)*
Tel 22 42 47 45   Fax 22 42 48 74

Poland
BTA, PO Box 15, 00-996 Warsaw 89

Portugal
BTA, Rua Luciano Cordeiro, 123, 2 Dt,
1050 Lisbon
Tel (1) 312 9020   Fax (1) 312 9030

Singapore
BTA, #01-01 Cecil Court, 138 Cecil Street,
Singapore 069 538
Tel (65) 227 5400   Fax (65) 227 5411

South Africa
BTA, Lancaster Gate, Hyde Park Lane,
Hyde Lane, Hyde Park, Sandton 2196 *(visitors)*
PO Box 41896, Craighall 2024 *(mail)*
Tel (11) 325 0343   Fax (11) 325 0344

Spain
BTA, Torre de Madrid 6/5, Plaza de España 18,
28008, Madrid
Tel (1) 541 13 96   Fax (1) 542 81 49

Sweden
BTA, Klara Norra, Kyrkogata 29,
S 111 22 Stockholm *(visitors)*
Box 3102, 103 62 Stockholm *(mail)*
Tel (8) 4401 700   Fax (8) 21 31 29

Switzerland
(Information Office only)
BTA, Limmatquai 78, CH-8001 Zurich
Tel (1) 261 42 77   Fax (1) 251 44 56

Taiwan
BTA, 7th Floor, Fu Key Building,
99 Jen Ai Road, Section 2, Taipei 10625
Tel (2) 351 0991   Fax (2) 392 6653

Thailand
BTA, 942/33 Ground Floor,
Charn Issara Tower, Rama IV Road, Bangkok,
10500 Thailand
Tel (2) 267 5077   Fax (2) 267 5078

USA (Chicago)
BTA, 625 N Michigan Avenue, Suite 1510,
Chicago IL 60611 *(personal callers only)*
Toll-free #1-800 462 2748

USA (New York)
BTA, 7th Floor, 551 Fifth Avenue, New York,
NY 10176-0799
Toll-free #1-800 GO 2 BRITAIN
or Tel (1) 212 986 2200

A BRIEF GUIDE TO THE
Welsh Language

In many parts of Wales visitors may hear Welsh spoken as an everyday language along with English. Here's a short introduction.

A Few Greetings

Welsh	English
Bore da	Good morning
Dydd da	Good day
Prynhawn da	Good afternoon
Noswaith dda	Good evening
Nos da	Good night
Sut mae?	How are you?
Hwyl	Cheers
Diolch	Thanks
Diolch yn fawr iawn	Thanks very much
Croeso	Welcome
Croeso i Gymru	Welcome to Wales
Da	Good
Da iawn	Very good
Iechyd da!	Good health!
Nadolig Llawen!	Merry Christmas!
Blwyddyn Newydd Dda!	Happy New Year!
Dymuniadau gorau	Best wishes
Cyfarchion	Greetings
Penblwydd hapus	Happy birthday

The Welsh National Anthem

Mae hen wlad fy nhadau yn annwyl i mi,
Gwlad beirdd a chantorion enwogion o fri;
Ei gwrol ryfelwyr, gwladgarwyr tra mad,
Dros ryddid collasant eu gwaed.

Chorus

Gwlad! Gwlad! Pleidiol wyf i'm gwlad;
Tra môr yn fur i'r bur hoff bau,
O bydded i'r hen iaith barhau.

———— ● ————

The ancient land of my fathers is dear to me,
A land of poets and minstrels, famed men.
Her brave warriors, patriots much blessed,
It was for freedom that they lost their blood.

Chorus

Homeland! I am devoted to my country;
So long as the sea is a wall to this fair beautiful land,
May the ancient language remain.

Pronunciation

There are some sounds in spoken Welsh which are very different from their English equivalents. Here's a basic guide.

Welsh		English equivalent
c	**c**ath *(cat)*	**c**at (never as in re**c**eive)
ch	**ch**waer *(sister)*	lo**ch**
dd	yn **dd**a *(good)*	**th**em
f	y **f**am *(the mother)*	o**f**
ff	**ff**enestr *(window)*	o**ff**
g	**g**ardd *(garden)*	**g**arden (never as in **G**eorge)
h	**h**et *(hat)*	**h**at (never silent as in **h**onest)
th	by**th** *(ever)*	**Th**ree (never as in **th**e)
ll	**ll**aw *(hand)*	There is no equivalent sound.

Place the tongue on the upper roof of the mouth near the upper teeth, ready to pronounce **l**; then blow rather than voice the **l**

The vowels in Welsh are **a e i o u w y**; all except **y** can be long or short:

long **a**	t**a**d *(father)*	similar to h**a**rd
short **a**	m**a**m *(mother)*	similar to h**a**m
long **e**	h**e**n *(old)*	similar to s**a**ne
short **e**	p**e**n *(head)*	similar to t**e**n
long **i**	m**i**s *(month)*	similar to g**ee**se
short **i**	pr**i**n *(scarce)*	similar to t**i**n
long **o**	m**ô**r *(sea)*	similar to m**o**re
short **o**	ff**o**n *(walking stick)*	similar to f**o**nd
long **w**	s**w**n *(sound)*	similar to m**oo**n
short **w**	g**w**n *(gun)*	similar to l**oo**k

y has two sounds:

1. Clear

d**y**n *(man)*	a long 'ee' sound almost like g**ee**se
c**y**n *(before)*	a short 'i' sound almost like t**i**n

2. Obscure –

something like the sound in English r**u**n, eg:

y *(the)*
yn *(in)*
d**y**nion *(men)*

It is well to remember that in Welsh the accent usually falls on the last syllable but one of a word, eg ca**d**air *(chair)*.

Publications, Guides and Maps

If you want more information on Wales you'll find it in this extensive range of publications.
Some are saleable, others are free.

FOR COPIES OF ALL GUIDES AND BROCHURES (FREE AND SALEABLE) PLEASE SEE THE COUPON OPPOSITE.

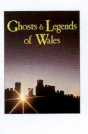

Wales – Bed and Breakfast is one of a series of three official 1998 'Where to Stay' guides in which all accommodation has been checked out by the Wales Tourist Board.

Wales – Hotels, Guest Houses and Farmhouses 1998 £3.95

A wide cross-section of accommodation, with a great choice of places to stay throughout Wales. Something for all tastes and pockets.

Wales – Self-Catering 1998 £3.75

Thousands of self-catering properties, including cottages, flats, chalets and caravan holiday home parks. Also a huge range of parks for touring caravans, motorhomes and tents.

The Complete Guides to South, Mid and North Wales £5.40 each

A best-selling series, written by Welsh author Roger Thomas. These three books give you the complete picture of Wales's holiday regions. In full colour – and packed with information. Fully revised and redesigned in new format for 1998.
• Descriptions of resorts, towns and villages
• Where to go and what to see
• Hundreds of attractions and places to visit
• Scenic drives, castles, crafts, what to do on a rainy day
• Detailed maps and town plans

Wales Tourist Map £2.35

A best-seller – and now better than ever. Detailed 5 miles/inch scale, fully revised and updated. Also includes suggested car tours, town plans, information centres.

All prices include postage and packing

A Journey Through Wales £5.10

A magnificent production – 64 big-format pages of the best images in Wales. The 90 photographs take the reader on a tour of Wales's mighty castles, spectacular mountains and coastline, country towns and colourful attractions.

Travelmaster Guide to South Wales £8.65

A new guide in the popular Travelmaster series. This 96-page book, written by Roger Thomas, contains 20 car tours plus information on what to see along the way. Includes the most accurate and up-to-date Ordnance Survey mapping.

Exploring Snowdonia, Anglesey and the Llŷn Peninsula £4.80

144 pages of detailed touring information, maps and illustrations. Discover the quietest roads and places to visit with this guide.

Ghosts and Legends of Wales £5.75

144 pages of fascinating stories, ancient and modern. Some of the happenings recounted may sound incredible, many will leave the reader wondering.

'By Car' Guides £2.40 each

• The Brecon Beacons
• The Pembrokeshire Coast
Two of the 32-page White Horse series. Attractive routes, maps and photographs – the ideal car touring guides to these beautiful parts of Wales.

Ordnance Survey Pathfinder Guides £9.65 each

• Brecon Beacons and Glamorgan Walks
• Pembrokeshire and Gower Walks
• Snowdonia Walks (including Anglesey/Llŷn Peninsula)
80-page books with detailed maps, colour illustrations and descriptions which guide you safely along attractive walking routes.

Free Publications

Activity Wales

Magazine on all kinds of activities, from abseiling to windsurfing. Lots of information on accredited activity centres and visitor attractions, events, news and articles by well-known personalities.

Beaches Guide

This 'Beautiful Beaches – Clean Seas' brochure lists Wales's most appealing beaches. Includes European Blue Flag and Tidy Britain Group Seaside Award beaches. Available April 1998.

Cycling Wales

Looking for a holiday on wheels? This brochure covers everything from gentle cycling to adventurous mountain biking. Suggested routes, details of cycle hire and cycling organisations.

Discovering Accessible Wales (holidays for disabled people)

A guide full of ideas and helpful information for people who may have impaired movement or are confined to a wheelchair. Covers everything from accommodation to activities.

Fishing Wales

This brochure, written by well-known anglers, is an essential guide to Wales's superb game and sea fishing. Information on venues, clubs, accommodation and tackle shops.

Freedom Holiday Parks Wales

Caravan Holiday Home Park accommodation in Wales is high on standards and value for money – as you'll see from this brochure which only lists parks graded for quality by the Wales Tourist Board.

Golfing Wales

Wales's golf courses rank amongst the best in the world. Novices and experts alike will find their ideal course with the help of this brochure, which also includes information on green fees and accommodation.

Wales Farm Holidays Map

Handy publication featuring bed and breakfast and self-catering accommodation at farmhouses throughout Wales.

Wales Touring Caravan and Camping

Detailed guide to Wales Tourist Board-inspected caravan and camping parks which welcome touring caravans, motorhomes and tents.

Walking Wales

Brochure on Britain's most popular leisure activity – and the best place in which to enjoy it. Suggested routes, maps, places to stay, carry-ahead and walking tour package information.

PLEASE COMPLETE AND SEND TO: WALES TOURIST BOARD, DEPT BB98, DAVIS STREET, CARDIFF CF1 2FU

SALEABLE PUBLICATIONS

Please enclose the appropriate remittance in the form of a cheque (payable to Wales Tourist Board) or postal/money order in £ sterling. All prices include post and packing.

☐ Wales – Hotels, Guest Houses & Farmhouses 1998	£3.95
☐ Wales – Self-Catering 1998	£3.75
☐ A Complete Guide to South Wales	£5.40
☐ A Complete Guide to Mid Wales	£5.40
☐ A Complete Guide to North Wales	£5.40
☐ Wales Tourist Map	£2.35
☐ A Journey Through Wales	£5.10
☐ Travelmaster Guide to South Wales	£8.65
☐ Exploring Snowdonia, Anglesey & the Llŷn Peninsula	£4.80
☐ Ghosts & Legends of Wales	£5.75

By Car' Guides:

☐ The Brecon Beacons	£2.40
☐ The Pembrokeshire Coast	£2.40

OS Pathfinder Guides:

☐ Brecon Beacons & Glamorgan Walks	£9.65
☐ Pembrokeshire & Gower Walks	£9.65
☐ Snowdonia Walks (including Anglesey/ Llŷn Peninsula)	£9.65

FREE PUBLICATIONS

☐ Activity Wales
☐ Beaches Guide (available April 1998)
☐ Cycling Wales
☐ Discovering Accessible Wales
☐ Fishing Wales
☐ Freedom Holiday Parks Wales
☐ Golfing Wales
☐ Wales Farm Holidays Map
☐ Wales Touring Caravan & Camping
☐ Walking Wales

Name (please print): ....

Address (please print): ....

.... Post Code: ....

Total remittance enclosed (if applicable): £ .... Cheque/PO or Money Order No: ....

Make payable to Wales Tourist Board (if applicable)

Maps of WALES

The maps which follow divide Wales into 12 sections, each with a slight overlap. The grid overlaying each map will help you find the resort, town or village of your choice. Please refer to the map and grid reference which appears alongside the names of each place listed in the 'Where to Stay' section of the guide.

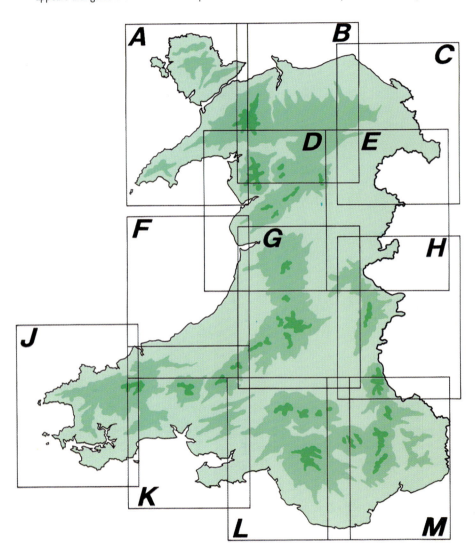

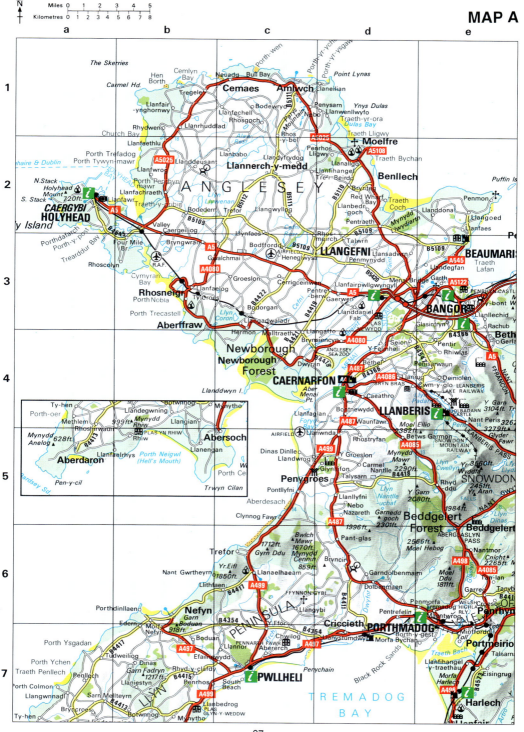

MAP B

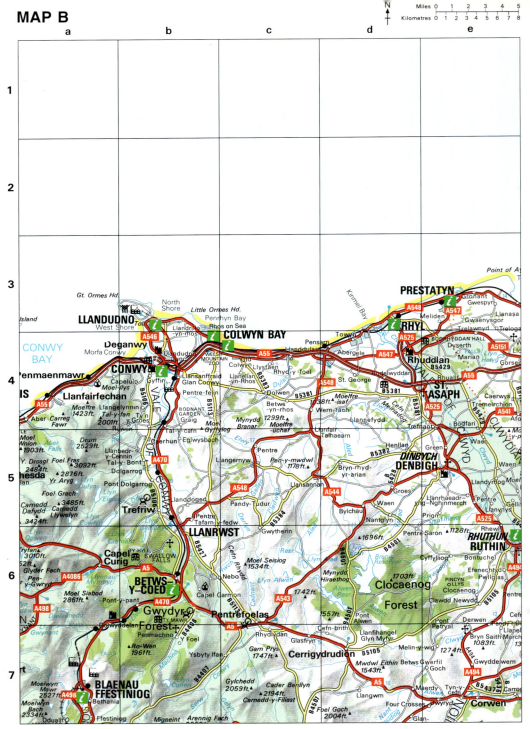

MAP C

Miles 0 1 2 3 4 5
Kilometres 0 1 2 3 4 5 6 7 8

N

a   b   c   d   e

Formby

Skelmersdale

Wi

A49

1

A565   A59   M58

A570

A49

A580   St. Helen's   N le-

Bootle   Liverpool

2

Wallasey   MERSEYSIDE   M57   A570   M62   Wa

Hoylake   Birkenhead   Widnes   A57

West Kirby   A41

Point of Ayr   Talacre

Heswell   Garston   Runcorn

3

DEE ESTUARY   Bebington   A533

Ffynnongroyw   B5126

Llanasa   A548   Mostyn   Neston   Ellesmere Port   Frodsham

Trelogan   Greenfield   M53   M56   12

A5151   Whitford BASINGWERK ABBEY   Lloc   HOLYWELL   A5117   Hapsford   A56

4

Gorsedd   A5026   Bagillt   A41

Brynford   FLINT   A548

Caerwys   Babell   Halkyn   Flint Mountain   CONNAH'S QUAY   A550   Saughall   A54

A541   Afonwen Lixwm   A55   A5119   B5126   Shotton   Chester   Kelsall

Nannerch   Northop   Queensferry   A548   A51   Tarvin

Rhydymwyn   Sychdyn   HAWARDEN AIRFIELD   CHESHIRE

5

Llys-y-coed   BUCKLEY   Hawarden   Tarporley

Moel Fammau   A549   Saltney   A41

A494   Gwernaffield   Broughton   A5118   Pen-y-ffordd

MOLD   A5104   Hope   Rossett   Trevalyn   A49

Clwyd Forest   Nercwys   Caergwrle

RUTHIN   Llanfynydd   Farndon

6

A494   Treuddyn   Cefn-y-bedd   A541   Gresford   Clutton

A5104   Rhydtalog   Brymbo   A534   Holt   Ridley Wood

A525   Bwlchgwyn   Broughton   Coed-poeth   No Man's Heath

Minera   Esclusham Mountain   WREXHAM   Malpas   A41

7

A542   Bryneglwys   Rhostyllen   B5130   A49

A5104   Ruabon   Bangor on Dee   Worthenbury   Higher Wych

Corwen   A5   Llangollen   VALLE CRUCIS ABBEY   Ruabon   Eyton   Overton   Penley   Eglwys Cross   Whit

A483   A525

MAP D

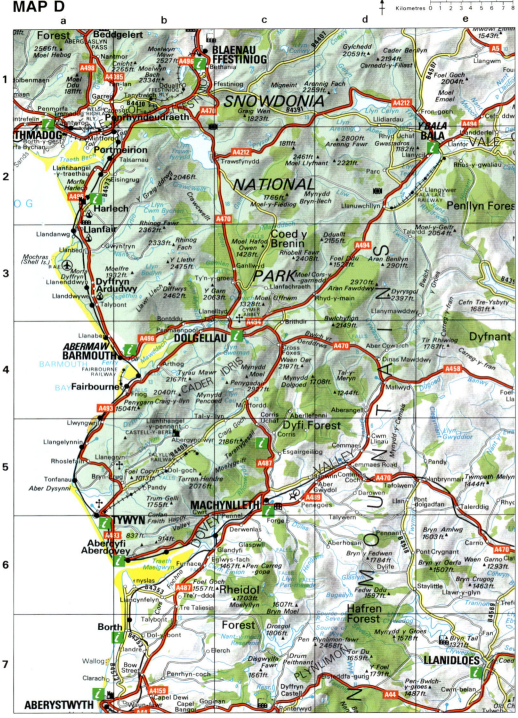

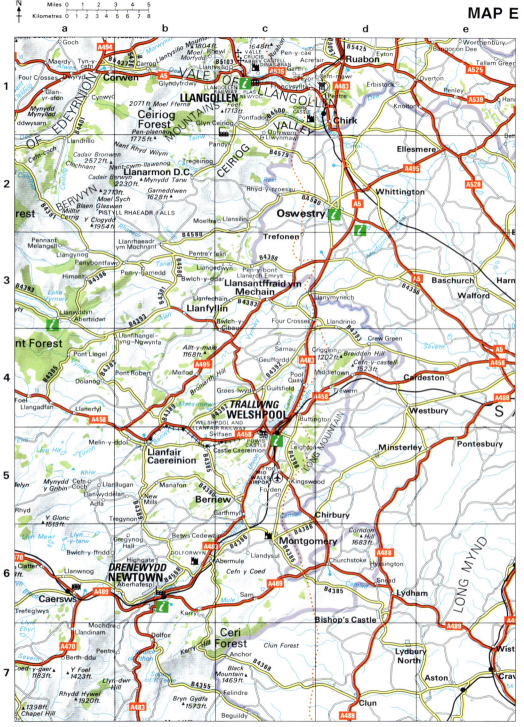

Miles 0 1 2 3 4 5
Kilometres 0 1 2 3 4 5 6 7 8

a   b   c   d   e

Row 1: Worthenbury, Bangor on Dee, Tallarn Green, Goch, Tyn-y-cefn, Maerdy, A494, B4436, Morwynion, Llantysilio Mountain, Moel Rhewl, 1804ft, 1648ft, Ruabon, B5425, Eyton, B5091, Pen-y-cae, Acrefair, B5103, VALE CRUCIS ABBEY, CASTELL DINAS BRAN, A535, Froncysyllte, Trevor, Cefn-mawr, A483, Erbistock, Overton, Penley, A539, Four Crosses, Glan-y-afon, Dwyryd, Corwen, A5, Glyndyfrdwy, LLANGOLLEN RAILWAY, PLAS NEWYDD, LLANGOLLEN, Pentre, Knolton, Chirk, CHIRK CASTLE, Dee, Ellesmere, A495

Row 2: Cynwyd, 2071ft Moel Fferna, Foel 1713ft, Pontfadog, Glyn Ceiriog, Dolywern & Llwynmawr, B4579, Rhyd-y-croesau, A483, A5, Whittington, A528, Ceiriog Forest, Pen-plaenau 1775ft, Pandy, Cadair Bronwen 2572ft, Clochnant, Nant Rhyd Wilym, Tregeinog, Llandrillo, Cefn-coch, Llanarmon D.C., Mynydd Tarw, Cadair Berwyn 2713ft, Gardeddwen 1628ft, Moelfre, Llansilin, Trefonen, Oswestry

Row 3: Mynydd Mynyllod, ddwysarn, BERWYN, Moel Sych 2713ft, Blaen Glaswen, Milltir Cerrig, Y Clogydd 1954ft, PISTYLL RHAEADR FALLS, Rhaeadr, Pennant Melangell, Llangynog, Penybontfawr, Hirnant, B4396, Pen-y-garnedd, B4580, Llanrhaeadr ym Mochnant, Pentre'r felin, Llangedwyn, B4396, Pen-y-bont, Llanerch Emrys, Llansantffraid ym Mechain, B4393, Llanfechain, Llanfyllin, Llanymynech, A5, Baschurch, Harl, Walford, B4396

Row 4: B4393, Lake Vyrnwy, Llanwddyn, Abertridwr, B4393, Bwlch-y-Cibau, Vyrnwy, Four Crosses, Llandrinio, B4393, Crew Green, Severn, A5, A458, Pont Llogel, Allt-y-main 1168ft, Sarnau, Geuffordd, Criggion, Breidden Hill 1202ft, Cefn-y-castell 1523ft, Pont Robert, Meifod, Broniarth Hill, A495, Groes-lwyd, Guilsfield, Pool Quay, Middletown, Trewern, Cardeston, A488, Dolanog, Llanerfyl, B4382, B4392, Westbury, S

Row 5: Llangadfan, Foel, A458, Maes-mawr, B4389, TRALLWNG WELSHPOOL, WELSHPOOL AND LLANFAIR RAILWAY, Sylfaen, Buttington, LONG MOUNTAIN, Minsterley, Pontesbury, Melin-y-ddol, Llanfair Caereinion, Castle Caereinion, A458, POWIS CASTLE, B4388, Leighton, Eunant, Llyn Hir, B4385

Row 6: Mynydd y Gribin, Cefn Coch, Llanllugan, Manafon, Afon Rhiw, Betws Cedewain, Berriew, MID WALES AIRPORT, Forden, Kingswood, Chirbury, Corndon Hill 1683ft, Montgomery, A488, Churchstoke, Hyssington, Lydham, A489, LONG MYND, New Mills, Adfa, Llanwyddelan, Rhyd, Y Glonc 1513ft, Llyn-y-tarw, Tregynon, Garthmyl, B4390, B4386, DOLFORWYN, Abermule, Llandysul, Cefn y Coed, A483, B4385, Snead, A489, Clatter, Bwlch-y-ffridd, Highgate, DRENEWYDD NEWTOWN, Aberhafesp, A489, Kerry, Sarn, Bishop's Castle, Lydbury North, Aston, A489, A4, Wist

Row 7: Caersws, A489, Llanwnog, Trefeglwys, Mochdre, Llandinam, Dolfor, Kerry Hill, Ceri Forest, Clun Forest, Anchor, Lydbury North, Aston, Crav, A470, Berth-ddu, Pentre, Source of Ithon, B4368, Black Mountain 1469ft, Clun, Coed-y-gaer 1183ft, Y Foel 1423ft, Rhyd Hywel, Llyn-dwr Hill 1920ft, B4355, Felindre, 1398ft, Chapel Hill, Bryn Gydfa 1573ft, Beguildy, A483, A488

MAP F

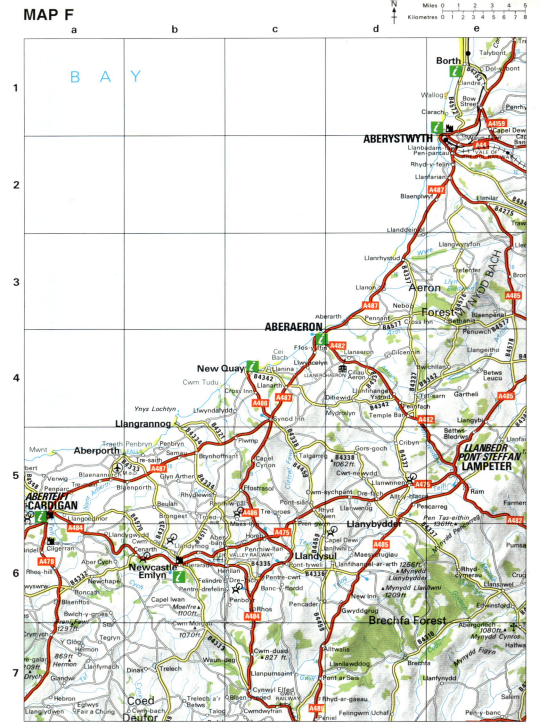

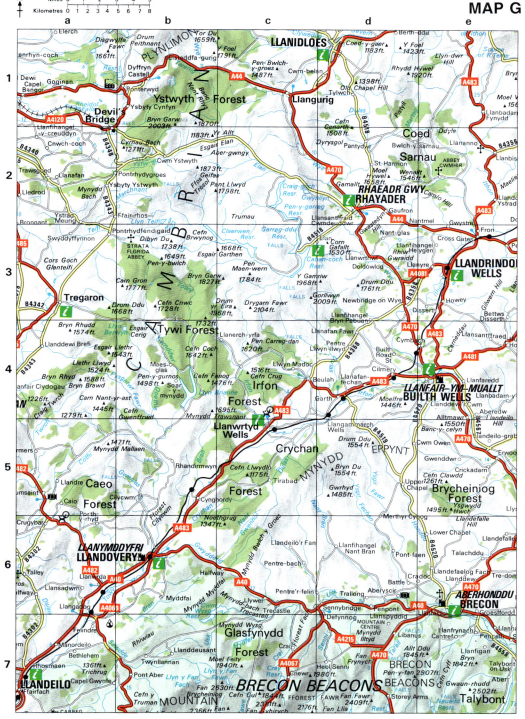

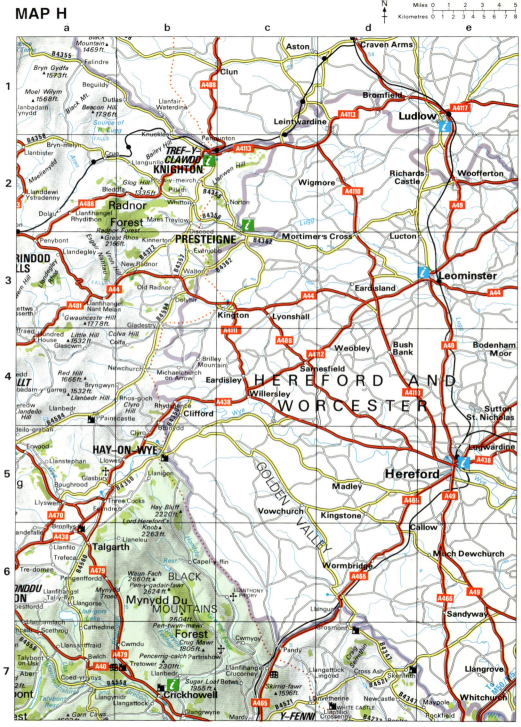

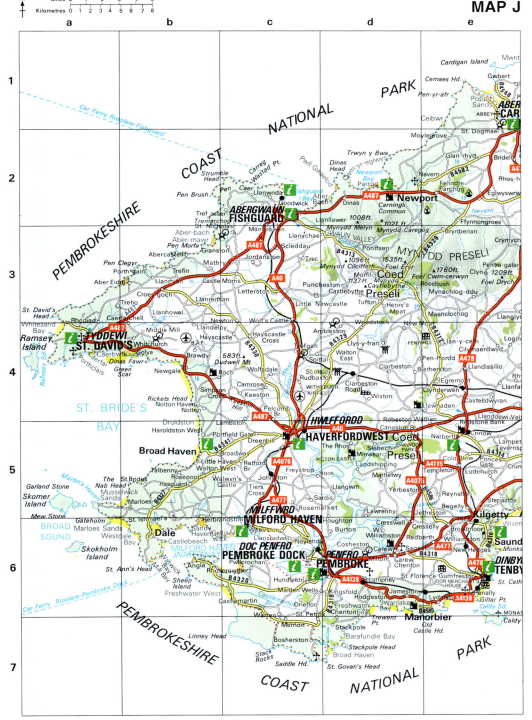

MAP K

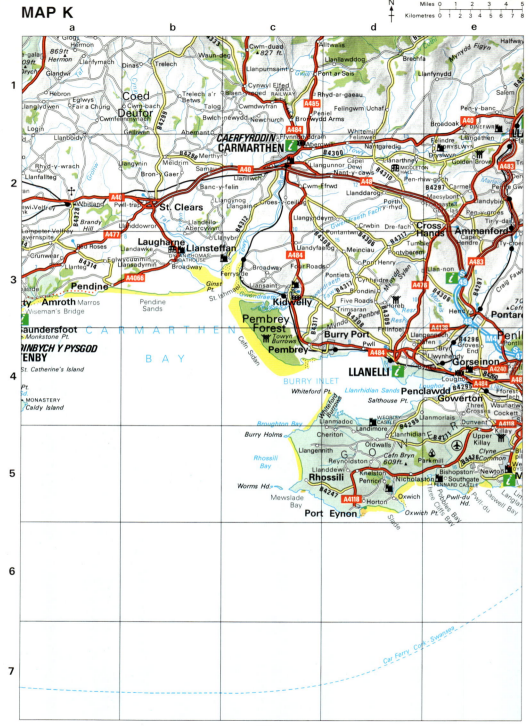

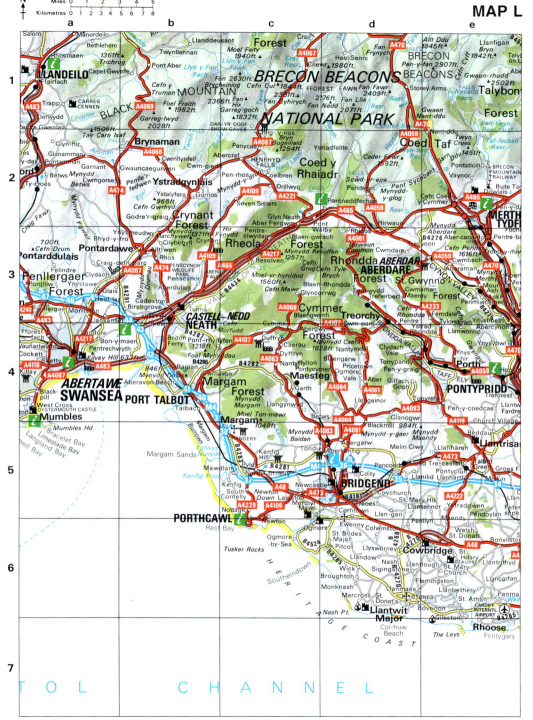

MAP L

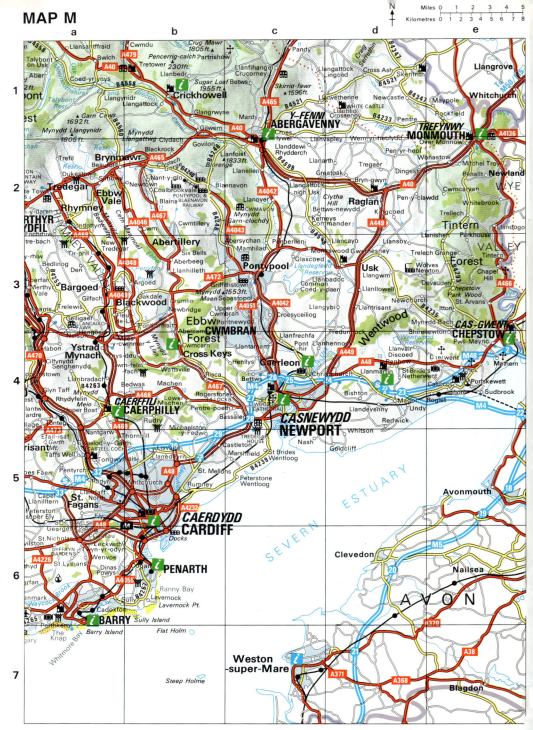